CAMBRIDGE PRIMARY
Mathematics

Challenge

6

Name: _____

Contents

Emma Low

CAMBRIDGE
UNIVERSITY PRESS

CAMBRIDGE
UNIVERSITY PRESS

University Printing House, Cambridge CB2 8BS, United Kingdom

One Liberty Plaza, 20th Floor, New York, NY 10006, USA

477 Williamstown Road, Port Melbourne, VIC 3207, Australia

4843/24, 2nd Floor, Ansari Road, Daryaganj, Delhi – 110002, India

79 Anson Road, #06–04/06, Singapore 079906

Cambridge University Press is part of the University of Cambridge.

It furthers the University's mission by disseminating knowledge in the pursuit of education, learning and research at the highest international levels of excellence.

www.cambridge.org
Information on this title: www.cambridge.org/9781316509258

First published 2016

20 19 18 17 16 15 14 13 12 11 10 9 8 7

Printed in Great Britain by CPI Group (UK) Ltd, Croydon CR0 4YY

A catalogue record for this publication is available from the British Library

ISBN 978-1-316-50925-8 Paperback

This book is part of the Cambridge Primary Maths project. This is an innovative combination of curriculum and resources designed to support teachers and learners to succeed in primary mathematics through best-practice international maths teaching and a problem-solving approach.

To get involved, visit
www.cie.org.uk/cambridgeprimarymaths.

Introduction

This *Challenge activity book* is part of a series of 12 write-in activity books for primary mathematics grades 1–6. It can be used as a standalone book, but the content also complements *Cambridge Primary Maths*. Learners progress at different rates, so this series provides a Challenge and Skills Builder activity book for each Primary Mathematics Curriculum Framework Stage to broaden the depth of and to support further learning.

The *Challenge* books extend learning by providing stretching activities to increase the depth of maths knowledge and skills. Support is given through short reminders of key information, topic vocabulary, and hints to prompt learning. These books have been written to support learners whose first language is not English.

How to use the books

The activities are for use by learners in school or at home, with adult support. Topics have been carefully chosen to focus on those areas where learners can stretch their depth of knowledge. The approach is linked directly to *Cambridge Primary Maths*, but teachers and parents can pick and choose which activities to cover, or go through the books in sequence.

The varied set of activities grow in challenge through each unit, including:

- closed questions with answers, so progress can be checked
- questions with more than one possible answer
- activities requiring resources, for example, dice, spinners or digit cards
- activities and games best done with someone else, in class or at home, which give the opportunity for parents and teachers to be fully involved in the child's learning
- activities to support different learning styles: working individually, in pairs, in groups
- A final section of problems and puzzles is provided to challenge learners at the end of Grade 6.

How to approach the activities

Space is provided for learners to write their answers in the book. Some activities might need further practice or writing, so students could be given a blank notebook at the start of the year to use alongside the book. Each activity follows a standard structure.

- **Remember** gives an overview of key learning points. It introduces core concepts and, later, can be used as a revision guide. These sections should be read with an adult who can check that the learner understands the material before attempting the activities.

- **Vocabulary** assists with difficult mathematical terms, particularly when English is not the learner's first language. Learners should read through the key vocabulary. Where necessary, they should be encouraged to clarify their understanding by using a mathematical dictionary or by, ideally, seeking adult help.

- **Hints** prompt and assist in building understanding, and steer the learner in the right direction.

- **You will need** gives learners, teachers and parents a list of resources for each activity.

- **Photocopiable resources** are provided at the end of the book, for easy assembly in class or at home.

- **Links** to the Cambridge International Examinations Primary Mathematics Curriculum Framework objectives and the corresponding *Cambridge Primary Mathematics Teacher's Resource* are given in the footnote on every page.

- **Calculators** should be used to help learners understand numbers and the number system, including place value and properties of numbers. From Stage 5, learners are expected to become proficient in using calculators in appropriate situations. This book develops the learner's knowledge of number without a calculator, although calculators can be useful for checking work.

Note:

When a 'spinner' is included, put a paperclip flat on the page so the end is over the centre of the spinner. Place the pencil point in the centre of the spinner, through the paperclip. Hold the pencil firmly and spin the paperclip to generate a result.

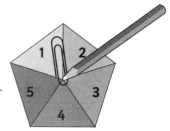

Tracking progress

Answers to closed questions are given at the back of the book – these allow teachers, parents and learners to check their work.

When completing each activity, teachers and parents are advised to encourage self-assessment by asking the students how straightforward they found the activity. When learners are reflecting on games, they should consider how challenging the mathematics was, not who won. Learners could use a ✓/ ✗ or red/green colouring system to record their self-assessment for each activity.

These assessments provide teachers and parents with an understanding of how best to support individual learners' next steps.

The number system

Remember
To solve these problems you need to understand that the position of a digit in a number is important to its value. Some of the positions are **millions**, **hundred thousands**, **ten thousands**, **thousands**, **hundreds**, **tens**, **ones**, **tenths**, **hundredths**, **thousandths**.

<, > and = are signs used to compare two values. < means 'less than', > means 'greater than', and = means 'equal to'.

You will need: resource 1, page 78

Vocabulary
million

1 Expand each of these numbers and shade the corresponding sections of the place-value chart. You will reveal a hidden number.

37005.92, 790 083.19, 251 030.75, 979 209.3, 10 857.57

100 000	200 000	300 000	400 000	500 000	600 000	700 000	800 000	900 000
10 000	20 000	30 000	40 000	50 000	60 000	70 000	80 000	90 000
1000	2000	3000	4000	5000	6000	7000	8000	9000
100	200	300	400	500	600	700	800	900
10	20	30	40	50	60	70	80	90
1	2	3	4	5	6	7	8	9
0.1	0.2	0.3	0.4	0.5	0.6	0.7	0.8	0.9
0.01	0.02	0.03	0.04	0.05	0.06	0.07	0.08	0.09

Use the place value chart below and/or resource 1 to make your own hidden word. Use numbers up to 1 million, with up to two decimal places.

100 000	200 000	300 000	400 000	500 000	600 000	700 000	800 000	900 000
10 000	20 000	30 000	40 000	50 000	60 000	70 000	80 000	90 000
1000	2000	3000	4000	5000	6000	7000	8000	9000
100	200	300	400	500	600	700	800	900
10	20	30	40	50	60	70	80	90
1	2	3	4	5	6	7	8	9
0.1	0.2	0.3	0.4	0.5	0.6	0.7	0.8	0.9
0.01	0.02	0.03	0.04	0.05	0.06	0.07	0.08	0.09

Give your numbers to a partner to expand and shade, to find your hidden word.

Unit 1A: Number and problem solving
CPM framework 6Nn2, 6Nn3, 6Nn8, 6Nn10, 6Nn12, 6Nn13, 6Pt5; Teacher's Resource 1.1, 1.2

2 Mark these numbers as accurately as you can on the number line.

| 2458 | | 5230 | | 9103 | | 7312 | | 1085 | | 9862 |

0 ──▶ 10 000

> **Hint:** Mark 'landmark' numbers such as 5000, on the line first.
> Round each number to the nearest 1000 or 100 to help position them on the number line.

3 Complete each number sentence with <, > or =.

986 577 ☐ 985 677   5 × 210 ☐ 150 × 7

9.23 + 8.69 ☐ 27.74 – 9.95   8.29 ☐ 8.3

8.45 × 100 ☐ 845 000 ÷ 100

4 Maria has carefully measured the amount of water she can store in one container.

12476 ml

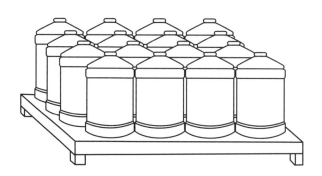

Approximately how much can she store in 16 containers?

Explain how you worked out your approximation, and why you think it is a good approximation.

> **Hint:** Try rounding the number. Try partitioning to multiply.

Unit 1A: Number and problem solving
CPM framework 6Nn2, 6Nn3, 6Nn8, 6Nn10, 6Nn12, 6Nn13, 6Pt5; Teacher's Resource 1.1, 1.2

5

Multiples, factors and primes

Remember

When a number is a multiple of two different numbers, it is a **common multiple** of the numbers, for example, 30 is a common multiple of 3 and 5.

A **prime number** has exactly two factors, itself and 1.

A **general statement** is a rule that always works.

You will need: calculator

Vocabulary
factor, multiple, prime

---

1 How many common multiples are there of 5 and 7 between 1 and 200?

There are ⬚ common multiples of 5 and 7 between 1 and 200.

The multiples are:

> **Hint:** Use known facts about recognising multiples of 5.
> Which numbers between 1 and 200 have the same property as multiples of 5?

2 Identify the three prime numbers in this grid.

81	82	83	84	85	86	87	88	89	90
91	92	93	94	95	96	97	98	99	100

Prime numbers: ⬚ , ⬚ , ⬚

Which numbers in this grid have the most factors? ⬚

Use this space to investigate.

Which numbers in this grid have an odd number of factors? Why?

> **Hint:** Find pairs of factors systematically, for example, is the number a multiple of 2?
> If it is what is 2 multiplied by to make the number? Is the number a multiple of 3?
> If it is then what is 3 multiplied by to make the number?

Unit 2A: Number and problem solving
CPM framework 6Nn6, 6Nn7, 6Nn17, 6Nn18, 6Nn19, 6Ps5; Teacher's Resource 12.1, 12.2, 13.1

3 Go through the maze to find the correct exit.

DO NOT solve the calculations, but work out whether the solution would be odd or even.

If the solution is even, turn right, if the solution is odd, turn left.

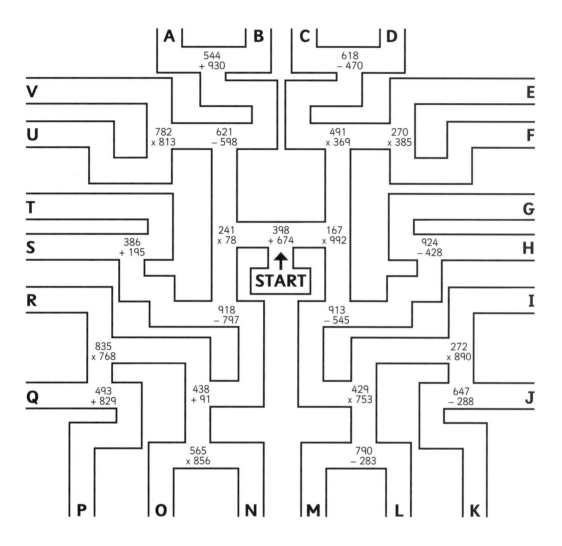

The correct maze exit is: ☐

Explain how you knew whether a solution would be even or odd.

For all of the calculations in the maze, write E next to it if the solution is even, and O if it is odd.

Unit 2A: Number and problem solving
CPM framework 6Nn6, 6Nn7, 6Nn17, 6Nn18, 6Nn19, 6Ps5; Teacher's Resource 12.1, 12.2, 13.1

7

4 What numbers between 1 and 40 can be made by adding pairs of consecutive prime numbers? Shade them on the grid.

1	2	3	4	5	6	7	8	9	10
11	12	13	14	15	16	17	18	19	20
21	22	23	24	25	26	27	28	29	30
31	32	33	34	35	36	37	38	39	40

What do you notice about the sums of consecutive prime numbers?

Write a general statement to describe the total when two consecutive prime numbers are added.

Hint: 7 and 11 are consecutive prime numbers. 11 is the next prime number after 7.

Unit 2A: Number and problem solving
CPM framework 6Nn6, 6Nn7, 6Nn17, 6Nn18, 6Nn19, 6Ps5; Teacher's Resource 12.1, 12.2, 13.1

5   Use the numbers 1 to 9 once in each grid.

Place the numbers so that the totals of each row and each column are all prime numbers.

How many different grids can you complete?

Hint: Use what you know about the sums of odd and even numbers to identify which sets of three numbers might total a prime number.

Unit 1A: Number and problem solving
CPM framework 6Nn4, 6Nc8, 6Nc10, 6Nc14, 6Nc15, 6Nc16; Teacher's Resource 3.1, 3.2, 4.2

9

Multiplication and division 1

Remember
To solve these problems you need to understand what happens to a number when it is multiplied or divided by 10, 100 or 1000.

A **remainder** is a whole number that is left over after division.

You will need: 30 counters in two different colours

Vocabulary
near multiple, remainder

1 Draw lines to match the boxes that produce the same answer for a number.

× 100

× 10 ÷ 1000

× 100 ÷ 1000

× 10 × 100

× 10 × 10 × 10

÷ 1000 × 10

÷ 10

× 10 × 10

× 100 ÷ 10

÷ 100 × 1000

Hint: Choose a number, for example, 5.
Work out what each of the boxes will do to that number.

Unit 1A: Number and problem solving
CPM framework 6Nn4, 6Nc8, 6Nc10, 6Nc14, 6Nc15, 6Nc16; Teacher's Resource 3.1, 3.2, 4.2

2 Find a route across the river on the stepping stones.

Only stepping stones with a calculation that leaves a remainder of 3 are safe.
Only move horizontally and vertically, no diagonal moves.

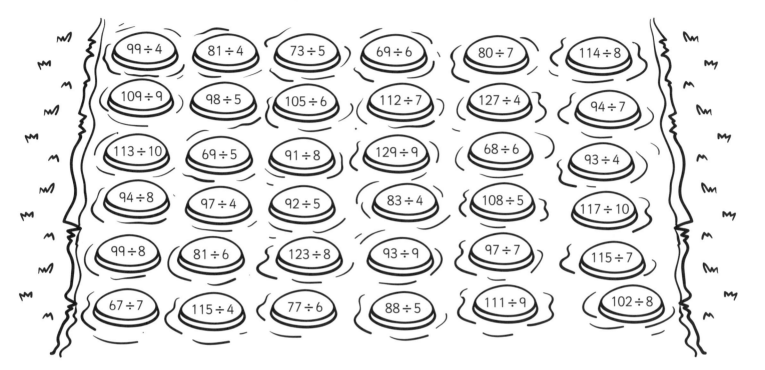

Use this space for your working.

Unit 1A: Number and problem solving
CPM framework 6Nn4, 6Nc8, 6Nc10, 6Nc14, 6Nc15, 6Nc16; Teacher's Resource 3.1, 3.2, 4.2

11

3 This is a game for two players.

Take turns to spin both spinners.
Find the product of the two numbers.

Put a counter on a square with the product
of the two numbers, unless all squares with
that number have already been covered.

The first player to get four counters in a
horizontal, vertical or diagonal line wins.

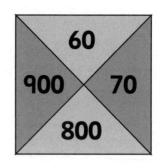 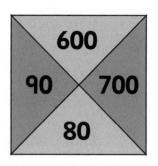

36 000	540 000	5400	81 000	42 000	4800
72 000	480 000	560 000	49 000	540 000	5600
64 000	6300	42 000	630 000	36 000	540 000
49 000	630 000	81 000	72 000	6300	42 000
5600	72 000	4800	64 000	5400	480 000

Hint: Use times tables facts and place-value knowledge
to multiply multiples of 10 and 100.

4 Estimate which of these will make the product closest to 2500. Mark it with an E.
Calculate each product to check.

37 × 6

48 × 51

21 × 13

79 × 29

Hint: Use rounding to the nearest 10 and adjusting to
find a quick estimate, then calculate the products.

Unit 1A: Number and problem solving
CPM framework 6Nn4, 6Nc8, 6Nc10, 6Nc14, 6Nc15, 6Nc16; Teacher's Resource 3.1, 3.2, 4.2

Number sequences

Remember

These mathematical sequences follow rules. The same rule is applied to each number in the sequence to make the next term.

A number line can be useful for working out the step size in a sequence.

You will need: ruler

Vocabulary

sequence, step, term, rule

1 Choose a two-digit whole number.

   Write the first eight terms of a sequence, starting on your number, that has the rule + 4.35.

   ▢ , ▢ , ▢ , ▢ , ▢ , ▢ , ▢ , ▢

   Use this space for calculating the terms.

   Will the 20th term have one or two decimal places? ▢

   Choose a three-digit whole number.

   Write the first eight terms of a sequence, starting on your number, that has the rule + 56.94.

   ▢ , ▢ , ▢ , ▢ , ▢ , ▢ , ▢ , ▢

   Use this space for calculating the terms.

   What will be the next term that has only one decimal place? ▢

   Hint: Look for patterns in the terms of the sequence.

2 Write a sequence with equal steps in which the third term is 1 and the fifth term is 2.5.

[ ] , [ ] , [ ] , [ ] , [ ]

What is the rule? [ ]

What is the 10th term? [ ]

> **Hint:** Start by working out what the fourth term must be.
> Drawing a number line and annotating with the steps could help.

3 Complete the sequence. The steps are equal.

$11\frac{1}{4}$, [ ] , [ ] , [ ] , [ ] , $13\frac{1}{8}$

What is the rule? [ ]

What would the 10th term of the sequence be? [ ]

> **Hint:** Draw a number line. Try different step sizes to get from $11\frac{1}{4}$ to $13\frac{1}{8}$ with five equal steps.

4 For each of these sequences, the rule is: halve it, then multiply by 3.
Work out the missing terms.

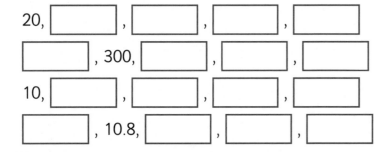

20, [ ] , [ ] , [ ] , [ ]

[ ] , 300, [ ] , [ ] , [ ]

10, [ ] , [ ] , [ ] , [ ]

[ ] , 10.8, [ ] , [ ] , [ ]

> **Hint:** Multiply numbers with decimals by 3 by adding the number three times, for example, 12.5 × 3 = 12.5 + 12.5 + 12.5.

Use this space for calculating the terms.

Unit 1A: Number and problem solving
CPM framework 6Nn15, 6Nc11, 6Ps5; Teacher's Resource 4.1, 4.3

Length

Remember

Millimetres, centimetres, metres and kilometres are metric units of length. Always record the units of measurement with your answer.

$1 \text{ km} = 1000 \text{ m} = 100\,000 \text{ cm} = 1\,000\,000 \text{ mm}$

$1 \text{ mm} = 0.1 \text{ cm} = 0.001 \text{ m} = 0.000\,001 \text{ km}$

You will need: ruler, protractor, string

Vocabulary

length, millimetre, centimetre, metre, kilometre

1   Draw two lines, at right angles, from the same point.
One line should be 7.3 cm long. The other line should be 4.6 cm long.

Join the ends of the lines to make a scalene triangle.

What is the length of the third side of the triangle?
Give your answer in millimetres, to the nearest mm.

Hint: Use a protractor or make a right angle checker to check that the two lines meet at a right angle.

2 Draw two different isosceles right angled triangles.
The triangles must have at least one side that is 6.5 cm long.

Label the lengths of the sides of the two triangles.

> **Hint:** An isosceles triangle has two sides that are the same length and two angles the same size.

3 A rope measuring 1.395 m is cut into five equal lengths.

How long is each piece, in cm? [ ]

Eight children in a team are taking part in a relay run.
The total race distance is 7.86 km. The race is divided so that each runner runs the same distance.

How many metres will each child run? [ ]

How many centimetres will each child run? [ ]

Unit 1B: Measure and problem solving
CPM framework 6MI1, 6MI2, 6MI4, 6Pt2; Teacher's Resource 5.1, 5.2

4 The circumference of a circle is its perimeter.

Measure the circumference of this circle.
Give your answer to the nearest centimetre.

Hint: Place string over the circumference of the circle, then measure the string.

5 Erik says: 'The circumference of a circle is approximately three times the widest distance across the circle.'

Use these circles to investigate whether Erik is correct.

Erik is correct / incorrect because ...

Hint: Measure the width and circumference of each circle as accurately as you can.

Timetables and calendars

You will need: calendar, timetables

Remember

To solve these problems you need to understand the units used for time, including years, months, weeks, days, hours, minutes and seconds.

You can draw a time line and use it like a number line to work out time intervals.

Vocabulary

12-hour clock, 24-hour clock, analogue, digital, am, pm, second, minute, hour, day, week, fortnight, month, year, decade, century

1 Today is the 8th day of the month. It is a Saturday.
Last month the 8th day was on a Thursday.
Next month the 8th day is on a Tuesday.

There are two possible dates it could be. What are they?

_____

> **Hint:** Work out how many days must have been in the last month and this month to make the 8th fall on those days.

2 Today is the 23rd day of the month. It is a Wednesday.
Last month the 23rd day was on a Tuesday.
Next month the 23rd day is on a Saturday.

What is the date today?

_____

3 Here is a page from a calendar for the year 2027.

Use the calendar and what you know about years, months, weeks and days to work out the day of the week on:

a) 1st August 2027 _____

b) 30th November 2027 _____

c) 1st January 2028 _____

d) 7th March 2028 _____

e) 31st December 2026 _____

13th September 2027 is on a Monday. Which is the next month after this that the 13th will be on a Monday? _____

> **Hint:** Remember to work out which years are leap years.

Unit 1B: Measure and problem solving
CPM framework 6Mt1, 6Mt4, 6Mt5, 6Mt6, 6Mt7, 6Pt2, 6Ps2; Teacher's Resource 6.1, 6.2

4 Six people are at a railway station waiting for six trains to different destinations.

Use the clues to work out the destination of each train.

Destination	Departure time
	11:48
	12:18
	12:58
	13:23
	13:53
	14:28

Clues

The train for Barcelona leaves later than the train for Brussels, but before the train for Venice.

The train for Brussels leaves between 12 o'clock and 1 o'clock.

The train for Vienna leaves later than the train for Copenhagen, but before the train for Barcelona.

The train to Vienna leaves 40 minutes before the next train.

The train that leaves at 7 to 2 is going to a place with six letters in its name.

The train for Warsaw leaves before the train for Venice but later than the train for Barcelona.

> **Hint:** Use this logic table to work out which train left when.
> Put a cross in any places that cannot be the correct time for that train. Tick the time when you know it is correct for that train.

	11:48	12:18	12:58	13:23	13:53	14:28
Barcelona						
Venice						
Brussels						
Vienna						
Warsaw						
Copenhagen						

Unit 1B: Measure and problem solving
CPM framework 6Mt1, 6Mt4, 6Mt5, 6Mt6, 6Mt7, 6Pt2, 6Ps2; Teacher's Resource 6.1, 6.2

19

5 Make your own timetable. Use 24-hour clock times.

There are five stations on the line. You can name the stations.
There are three trains. They can go back and forth along the line as many times as you like.
These are the times between stations:

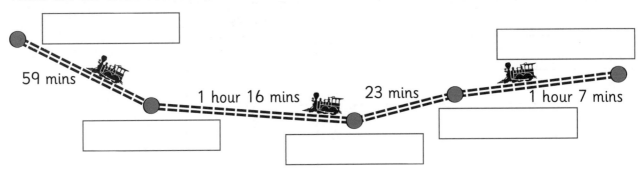

59 mins   1 hour 16 mins   23 mins   1 hour 7 mins

Trains must stop at each station for 2 minutes.

At the end of the line the train stops for 18 minutes before going back.

From [   ] to [   ] :

From [   ] to [   ] :

> **Hint:** Look at other bus or train timetables for ideas.
> Write the arrival and departure times from the first station to
> the fifth station in the first table.
> Write the arrival and departure times times from the fifth station
> back to the first station in the second table.

Unit 1B: Measure and problem solving
CPM framework 6Mt1, 6Mt4, 6Mt5, 6Mt6, 6Mt7, 6Pt2, 6Ps2; Teacher's Resource 6.1, 6.2

Polygons

Remember

A **polygon** has three or more straight sides. It is a closed 2D shape.

A kite has two pairs of **adjacent** (next to each other) sides that are the same length.

A **parallelogram** has both pairs of opposite sides **parallel**. **Rectangles** and **squares** are special parallelograms.

You will need:
protractor, ruler

Vocabulary
polygon, quadrilateral, parallelogram, rectangle, rhombus, square, trapezium, kite

1 Draw a shape in each section of the Venn diagram.

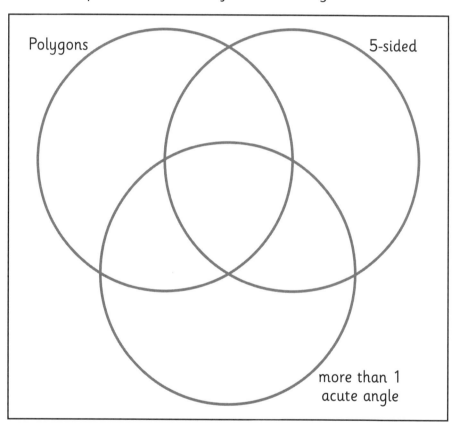

Polygons   5-sided

more than 1 acute angle

Hint: A shape with curved sides cannot be a polygon. Angles are made where two straight lines meet.

2 Investigate if it is possible to draw a kite with any pairs of parallel sides.

It is possible / is not possible to draw a kite with parallel sides.

Hint: Use a ruler to check that sides are parallel.

3 Investigate the relationship between the angles of a parallelogram.

Use these parallelograms first then draw some of your own to check your conclusions.

The angles of a parallelogram are ...

Hint: Measure and record the angles of the parallelograms.

Unit 1C: Geometry and problem solving
CPM framework 6Gs1, 6Gs3, 6Pt4; Teacher's Resource 8.1

3D shapes and nets

Remember

Polyhedra have polygonal faces. These 3D shapes have **faces** (flat polygon surfaces), **edges** (the lines, or folds, where the edges meet), and **vertices** (the points where the edges meet).

A 3D shape can be made by making a **net** and folding it along the edges.

You will need: resource 2, pages 79–83, solid cube, crayons, scissors

Vocabulary

polyhedron, face, edge, vertex, vertices, prism, pyramid

1   Use three colours to shade this net so that when it is folded no same colour faces will share an edge.

What shape will the net make? [   ]

What is the least number of colours you need to colour the faces of each of these shapes so that no same colour faces share an edge?

triangular prism [   ]   hexagonal prism [   ]

cuboid [   ]   heptagonal prism [   ]

pentagonal prism [   ]

Explain how you can reliably predict the least number of colours for each shape.

_____

_____

Hint: Colour and cut out the nets in resource 2 to test how many colours are needed. Make a table to compare the number of faces on the prism and the number of colours.

2 Use the least number of colours to shade this net so that when it is folded no same colour faces will share an edge.

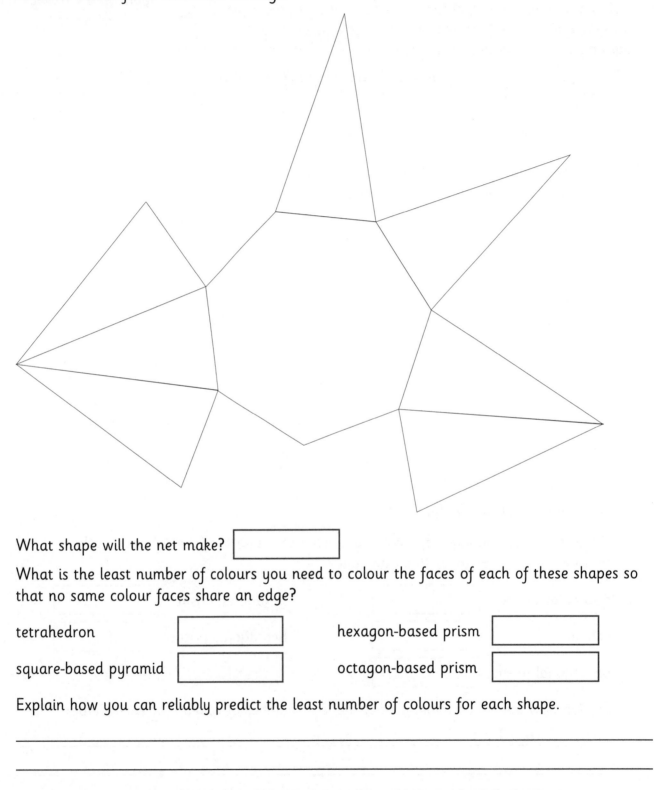

What shape will the net make? [   ]

What is the least number of colours you need to colour the faces of each of these shapes so that no same colour faces share an edge?

tetrahedron [   ]   hexagon-based prism [   ]

square-based pyramid [   ]   octagon-based prism [   ]

Explain how you can reliably predict the least number of colours for each shape.

_____

_____

_____

Hint: You can use the nets in resource sheet 2 to check your answers.

Unit 1C: Geometry and problem solving
CPM framework 6Gs2, 6Gs4, 6Pt4; Teacher's Resource 8.2, 8.3

3 Complete each row of the table with the name of one shape that has the given number of vertices.

Number of vertices	Shape
4	
5	
6	
7	
8	
9	
10	

4 Look at a real cube.

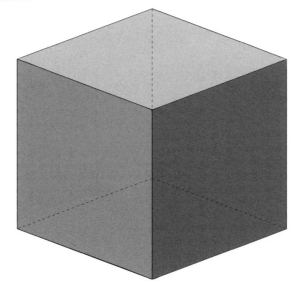

Imagine it is cut into two parts with a straight cut.

What shape faces could the two new 3D shapes have? Find five.

_____   _____   _____

_____   _____

Describe to a partner or adult how each of the face shapes could be made.

Hint: Try to visualise the cut and the two 3D shapes that are made.

Angles in a triangle

You will need: protractor, ruler

Remember

The sum of the **angles of a triangle** is 180°.

The sum of **angles on a straight line** is 180°.

Use ° to show that the angle measurement is in **degrees**.

Triangles can be **equilateral**, **isosceles** or **scalene**.

Vocabulary
angle, degrees

1   Complete the two properties of an equilateral triangle.

    A   All of the sides are ...

    B   All of the angles are ...

    Could the angles of an equilateral triangle be an angle other than 60°?

    Investigate.

    Give your answer and reasoning.

2   Draw a horizontal line 6 cm long.
    This is one side of a triangle.

    Make the angles at the ends of
    the line 48° and 64°.

    Join the angles to make a triangle.

    The sum of the angles should be ⬚ ,

    so the third angle should be ⬚ .

    Measure the third angle to see how accurately
    you have drawn and measured the angles.

    The third angle measures ⬚ .

> **Hint:** If the third angle does not match your calculation,
> measure again and draw the first two angles.

Unit 1C: Geometry and problem solving
CPM framework 6Gs5, 6Gs6, 6Pt4; Teacher's Resource 9.1

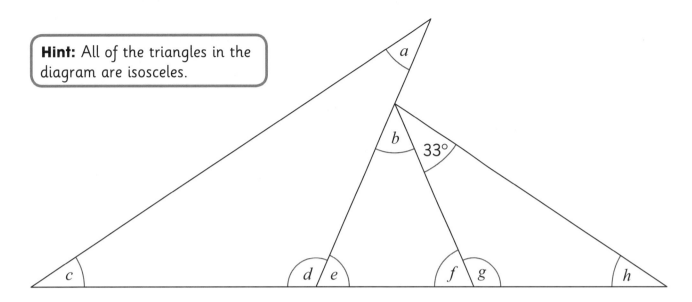

Hint: All of the triangles in the diagram are isosceles.

3 Estimate the size of the missing angles on this diagram.

(a) acute / obtuse. Estimate [   ]

(b) acute / obtuse. Estimate [   ]

(c) acute / obtuse. Estimate [   ]

(d) acute / obtuse. Estimate [   ]

(e) acute / obtuse. Estimate [   ]

(f) acute / obtuse. Estimate [   ]

(g) acute / obtuse. Estimate [   ]

(h) acute / obtuse. Estimate [   ]

Calculate the missing angles.

(a) [   ]   **(b)** [   ]

(c) [   ]   **(d)** [   ]

(e) [   ]   **(f)** [   ]

(g) [   ]   **(h)** [   ]

Hint: When calculating the missing angles it would be useful to start with g and h.

Transforming shapes

You will need: ruler, protractor or right angle checker, mirror or tracing paper (optional)

Vocabulary

coordinates, quadrants, x-axis, y-axis, translation, reflection, rotation, image, clockwise, anti-clockwise

1   Plot the points (–2, 6) and (–2, –6) on the grid.

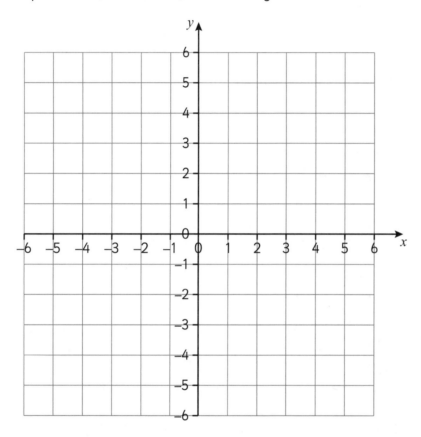

Draw a line between the points. Use a ruler. This is the mirror line.

Draw a triangle with these coordinates at the corners: (–4, 2.5), (–3, –2.5), (–5, –3.5).

Reflect the triangle over your mirror line.

What are the coordinates of the vertices of the reflected triangle?

Hint: Plot coordinates with decimals in the same way as whole-number coordinates. To mark the point that is 2.5 along the *y*-axis, find the halfway point between 2 and 3.

Unit 1C: Geometry and problem solving, **Unit 3C:** Geometry and problem solving
CPM framework 6Gp1, 6Gp2; Teacher's Resource 10.1, 10.2, 10.3, 34.2

2 Plot (–6, 4) on the grid.

Plot (6, –2) on the grid.

Draw a line between the points.
Use a ruler.

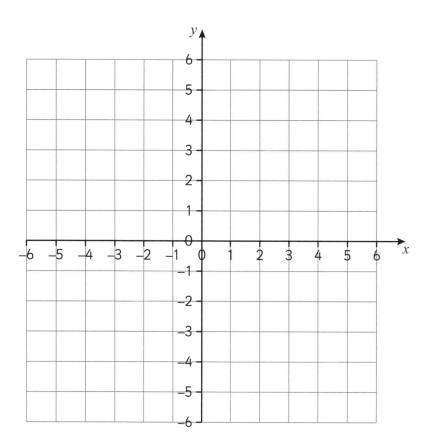

Write down the coordinates of three more points on the line.

⬚ , ⬚ , ⬚

Plot (–3, –5) on the grid.

Draw a line from (–3, –5) that is perpendicular to the first line.

Complete the coordinates:

The perpendicular line goes through (2, ⬚)

Plot the points (4, –1), (1, –2) and (3, 2) and join them to make a triangle.

Rotate and draw the triangle 90° clockwise about the point (0, 1).

Repeat until there are four triangles.

The triangles together make a small and a large square.

What are the coordinates of the corners of the large square?

⬚ , ⬚ , ⬚ , ⬚

Hint: Perpendicular lines meet at 90°. Use the perpendicular lines to help you rotate the triangle.

Unit 1C: Geometry and problem solving, Unit 3C: Geometry and problem solving
CPM framework 6Gp1, 6Gp2; Teacher's Resource 10.1, 10.2, 10.3, 34.2

29

3 Translate the shapes.

Shape A: translate −3 along the x-axis and +4 along the y-axis.

Shape B: translate +5 along the x-axis and +3 along the y-axis.

Shape C: translate −4 along the x-axis and −3 along the y-axis.

Shape D can be translated to complete a quadrilateral with the translations of A, B and C. Describe the translation.

Shape D translates ☐ along the x-axis and ☐ along the y-axis.

What is the name of the quadrilateral? ☐

What are the coordinates of the corners of the quadrilateral?

☐ , ☐ , ☐ , ☐

> **Hint:** Translate each corner of the shape and then join the translated points to make the translated shape. The translated shape should be the same size and shape as the original.

Unit 1C: Geometry and problem solving, Unit 3C: Geometry and problem solving
CPM framework 6Gp1, 6Gp2; Teacher's Resource 10.1, 10.2, 10.3, 34.2

Decimals and negative numbers

Remember

To solve these problems you need to understand that the position of a digit in a number is important to its value. Some of the positions are thousands, hundreds, tens, ones, tenths, hundredths, thousandths.

You have **strategies** to calculate addition, subtraction, multiplication and division with **decimals**.

You can draw a number line that includes **negative numbers** to help you solve problems involving negative and positive numbers.

You will need: 20 small blank cards, stopwatch or clock with a second hand

Vocabulary
positive, negative

1 The labels have fallen off the bottles. Match the correct label to each bottle.

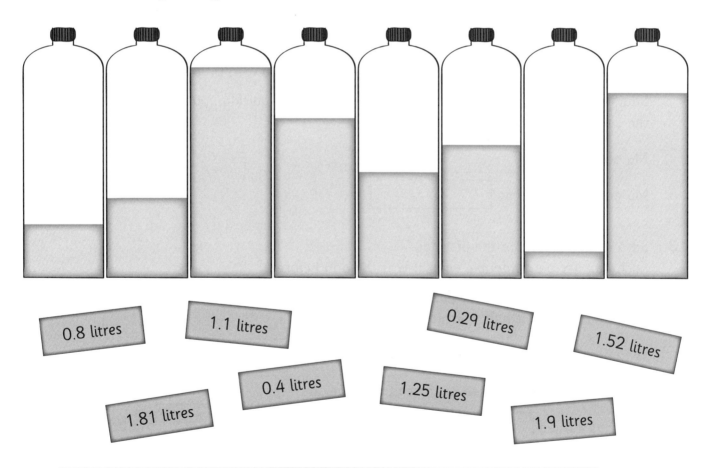

0.8 litres

1.1 litres

0.29 litres

1.52 litres

0.4 litres

1.25 litres

1.81 litres

1.9 litres

> **Hint:** Compare and order the amount of liquid in each bottle and compare the numbers on the labels. You could number the bottles first according to the volume of liquid in each, or write the labels in order, from lowest to greatest.

Unit 2A: Number and problem solving
CPM framework 6Nn3, 6Nn11, 6Nn14, 6Nc1, 6Nc2, 6Nc11, 6Nc12, 6Pt3; Teacher's Resource 12.1, 12.2, 13.1

31

2 Addition and subtraction facts

Find the pairs of numbers that total 1. Draw a line between them.

| 0.97 | 0.8 | 0.7 | 0.3 | 0.25 |

| 0.13 | 0.85 | 0.1 | 0.4 | 0.2 |

| 0.75 | 0.87 | 0.6 | 0.42 | 0.69 |

| 0.58 | 0.9 | 0.03 | 0.31 | 0.15 |

Write these numbers onto cards: 0.06, 0.16, 0.2, 0.24, 0.26, 0.3, 0.38, 0.4, 0.48, 0.49, 0.51, 0.52, 0.6, 0.62, 0.7, 0.74, 0.76, 0.8, 0.84, 0.94.

Shuffle the cards. Take turns with a partner to see how quickly you can sort the cards into pairs that equal 1.

My best time [   ] .

My partner's best time [   ] .

3 Sara is paid $0.90 on the first day.
Each day her pay is double what it was the day before.

Aisha is paid $57.60 on the first day.
Each day her pay is half what it was the day before.

Who has earned more at the end of two days? [   ]

How much has each earned at the end of eight days? [   ]

Sara has earned [   ] .

Aisha has earned [   ] .

> **Hint:** Remember that doubling is the same as multiplying by 2 and halving is dividing by 2. Round and estimate to check that answers are reasonable.

Unit 2A: Number and problem solving
CPM framework 6Nn3, 6Nn11, 6Nn14, 6Nc1, 6Nc2, 6Nc11, 6Nc12, 6Pt3; Teacher's Resource 12.1, 12.2, 13.1

4 These people have been trying to measure the depth of a hole. Unfortunately they have dropped the tape measure down the hole and they cannot get it out!

They managed to measure the hole by connecting some of these sticks together and found that its depth was 2.6 m.

Which combination of sticks could they have used?

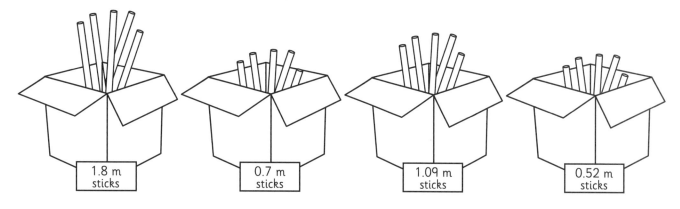

| 1.8 m sticks | 0.7 m sticks | 1.09 m sticks | 0.52 m sticks |

Hint: Try adding and/or multiplying the lengths of the sticks.
Work systematically to find out which sticks could **not** have been used.

Unit 2A: Number and problem solving
CPM framework 6Nn3, 6Nn11, 6Nn14, 6Nc1, 6Nc2, 6Nc11, 6Nc12, 6Pt3; Teacher's Resource 12.1, 12.2, 13.1

33

5 Four children played a game. They each started at 10 and took turns to roll a dice.
Each number they rolled was subtracted from their score.
These are the scores at the end of 10 rolls.

Name	Score
Safdar	−29
Natasha	−18
Ben	−33
Isobel	−31

Put the scores in order, from greatest to least. Write your results in this table.

Name	Score

Draw 10 dice to show what Isobel could have thrown to achieve her score.

6 Play the game from question 5 in a group of four.

Complete the table with the scores in order, from greatest to least.

Name	Score

> **Hint:** Draw a number line to help work out the scores.

Complete these sentences.

The difference between my score and _____ score equals [   ] .

The difference between my score and _____ score equals [   ] .

The difference between my score and _____ score equals [   ] .

Unit 2A: Number and problem solving
CPM framework 6Nn3, 6Nn11, 6Nn14, 6Nc1, 6Nc2, 6Nc11, 6Nc12, 6Pt3; Teacher's Resource 12.1, 12.2, 13.1

Mental strategies

Remember
It is easier to calculate if you know the **times tables**.
Look at the numbers in a calculation to choose the most efficient mental strategy.

Some mental strategies are:
- using place value, for example, use 32 + 65 to solve 320 + 650, or 3.2 + 6.5
- adding or subtracting near multiples of 10, 100 or 1000 by adding or subtracting the rounded number, then adjusting
- multiplying near multiples of 10 by multiplying by the rounded number, then adjusting
- multiplying by **halving** one number and **doubling** the other, for example, 36 × 18 = 72 × 9.

You will need:
counters, five each of two colours

Vocabulary
near multiple

1   This is a game for two players.

96	102	108	112
114	119	126	128
131	133	136	144
152	153	162	171

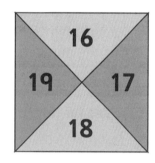
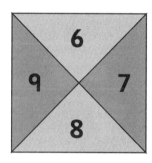

Both players need five counters of their own colour.

Spin both spinners. Both players quickly find the product of the two numbers. The first player to correctly identify the product places one of their counters on it, on the grid.

The first player to cover five numbers on the grid is the winner.

Hint: Use partitioning to multiply mentally quickly, for example, 16 × 8 = (10 × 8) + (6 × 8).

Unit 2A: Number and problem solving
CPM framework 6Nc4, 6Nc6, 6Nc8, 6Nc14, 6Nc15, 6Nc16, 6Nc17, 6Nc22, 6Pt1, 6Ps1; Teacher's Resource 14.1, 14.3

35

2 One of the numbers in activity 1 can be made in two different ways.

Which number is it? [   ]

How can it be made? [   ] × [   ] and [   ] × [   ]

One of the numbers in the game above is not a product of the numbers on the spinners.
Use this space to investigate.

Which number? [   ]

> **Hint:** Investigate systematically to find the number that is not a product of the numbers on the spinners.

3 Use quick mental strategies for multiplication.

89 × 7 = [   ]   6 × 71 = [   ]

60 × 800 = [   ]   17 × 7 = [   ]

24 × 66 = [   ]   84 × 35 = [   ]

900 × 400 = [   ]   8 × 27 = [   ]

Explain to a partner what strategies you used to calculate the answers quickly.

> **Hint:** Consider partitioning, multiplying by a multiple of 10 and adjusting or halving one number and doubling the other as mental strategies.

Unit 2A: Number and problem solving
CPM framework 6Nc4, 6Nc6, 6Nc8, 6Nc14, 6Nc15, 6Nc16, 6Nc17, 6Nc22, 6Pt1, 6Ps1; Teacher's Resource 14.1, 14.3

4   Draw lines from two bags to each box, to make the total mass written on the box.

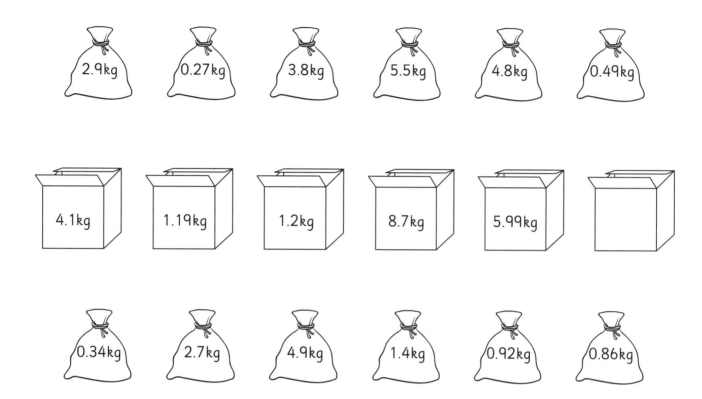

Label the last box with the total of the remaining two bags.

Use this space for your working.

Hint: Use place value and number facts to add the masses on
pairs of bags, or subtract masses on different bags from the totals.
Work systematically, and record which bags have been tried.

Multiplication and division 2

Vocabulary

multiple, multiplication, divisible, divisibility

Remember

A **test of divisibility** shows if one number is a multiple of another, for example, to test for divisibility by 5 check whether the number ends in a 0 or 5.

To solve these problems you need to use some written methods for multiplying and dividing numbers.

1   In this game, you can only travel through numbers that are divisible by 4 with no remainders.
   You can only move horizontally or vertically, not diagonally.
   Which tent has a path to the mountain?

Hint: Apply tests of divisibility by 4 to each number on your path.

Tent A	512	460	724	106	398	714	282	538	162	804	970	598	896	732	364	192	Tent B
338	898	954	608	966	216	540	352	184	928	772	630	862	520	386	822	426	974
422	396	172	416	754	392	710	218	790	462	448	852	202	556	936	184	368	740
366	484	702	612	294	104	592	388	208	812	302	688	930	800	774	618	432	550
620	544	986	652	886	242	720	446	906	242	874	992	314	646	114	822	164	374
146	350	222	340	776	418	640	326			762	580	484	944	312	750	792	836
738	408	176	802	460	646	256	824			410	818	732	278	676	238	810	232
268	756	954	514	744	556	334	490	502	254	708	942	152	186	872	562	478	520
532	222	574	244	134	848	128	586	122	188	860	376	606	994	496	116	968	364
664	140	352	956	472	778	500	918	278	980	846	932	362	508	194	850	182	254
726	218	434	894	768	834	896	758	336	444	754	220	484	900	766	920	568	604
Tent C	628	420	292	300	266	280	908	616	998	406	362	174	780	324	884	526	Tent D

Unit 2A: Number and problem solving
CPM framework 6Nn4, 6Nc3, 6Nc10, 6Nc18, 6Nc19; Teacher's Resource 15.1, 15.2, 15.3

2 Use the numbers from the circles to complete the two number sentences so that they are true.

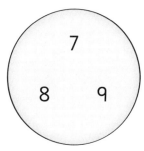
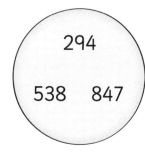

7

8   9

294

538   847

4304

4114   4274

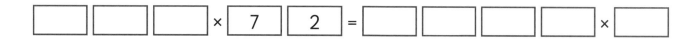

☐☐☐ × ⟨7⟩⟨2⟩ = ☐☐☐☐ × ☐

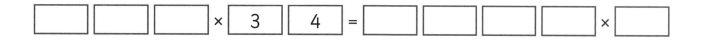

☐☐☐ × ⟨3⟩⟨4⟩ = ☐☐☐☐ × ☐

Write a number sentence using your own choice of numbers, but do not use multiples of 10.

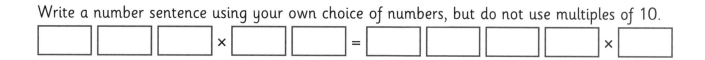

☐☐☐ × ☐☐ = ☐☐☐☐ × ☐

Hint: Do not use any of the same numbers in the two solutions.
Use the spaces for written calculations.

Unit 2A: Number and problem solving
CPM framework 6Nn4, 6Nc3, 6Nc10, 6Nc18, 6Nc19; Teacher's Resource 15.1, 15.2, 15.3

39

3 For each of these numbers, find a one-digit divisor so that the quotient will have a remainder of 5.

781 ÷ ☐ = ☐ remainder 5

782 ÷ ☐ = ☐ remainder 5

785 ÷ ☐ = ☐ remainder 5

788 ÷ ☐ = ☐ remainder 5

Use this space for your written calculations.

Find two solutions for:

789 ÷ ☐ = ☐ remainder 5

789 ÷ ☐ = ☐ remainder 5

Hint: To leave a remainder of 5, the divisor must be greater than 5.

Unit 2A: Number and problem solving
CPM framework 6Nn4, 6Nc3, 6Nc10, 6Nc18, 6Nc19; Teacher's Resource 15.1, 15.2, 15.3

Mass and capacity

Remember
To solve these problems you need to be able to read a **scale** accurately. Work out what each unlabelled **division mark** on the scale stands for and remember to use the correct **units** for mass or capacity.

1 litre = 1000 ml	1000 g = 1 kg
0.1 litre = 100 ml	100 g = 0.1 kg
0.01 litre = 10 ml	10 g = 0.01 kg
0.001 litres = 1 ml	1 g = 0.001 kg

1   Each parcel is 465 g.
    Draw the needle on each scale to show the mass as accurately as you can.

Hint: Use a ruler to draw the needle on the scales.

2 Draw the same amount of liquid in each of these measuring cylinders. Mark them as accurately as you can.

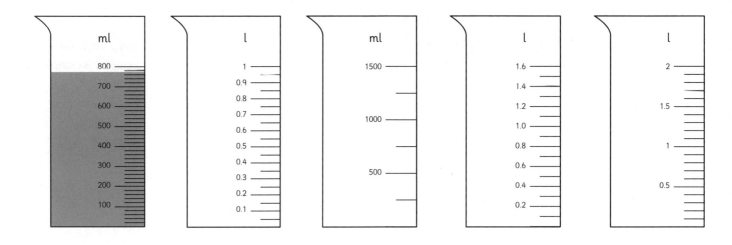

> **Hint:** Work out the amount of liquid in both litres and millilitres. Draw the level of liquid in each container with a ruler.

3 Find three different ways to use these containers to measure out exactly 2.74 litres.

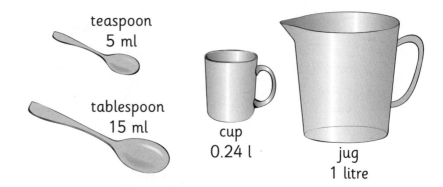

teaspoon
5 ml

tablespoon
15 ml

cup
0.24 l

jug
1 litre

Unit 2B: Measure and problem solving
CPM framework 6Ml1, 6Ml2, 6Ml3, 6Pt2, 6Ps7; Teacher's Resource 17.1, 17.2

4 This is a recipe for a healthy smoothie drink for one person.

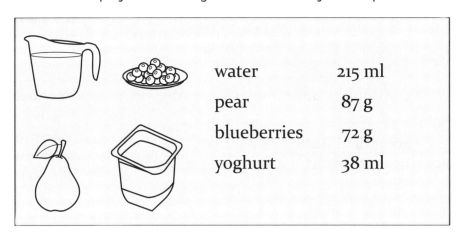

water	215 ml
pear	87 g
blueberries	72 g
yoghurt	38 ml

How much of each ingredient would be needed for 16 people? Take care converting the units!

water ☐ litres

pear ☐ kg

blueberries ☐ kg

yoghurt ☐ litres

Hint: Use a quick mental strategy to multiply by 16.

5 This is a recipe for a healthy smoothie drink for 24 people.

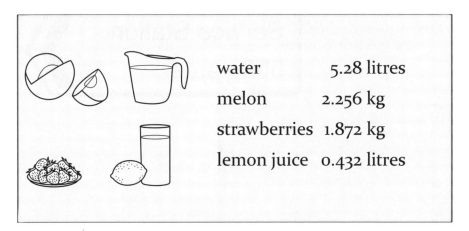

water	5.28 litres
melon	2.256 kg
strawberries	1.872 kg
lemon juice	0.432 litres

How much of each ingredient would be needed for two people? Take care converting the units!

water ☐ ml

melon ☐ g

strawberries ☐ g

lemon juice ☐ ml

Hint: Use a quick mental strategy to divide by 12.

Unit 2B: Measure and problem solving
CPM framework 6MI1, 6MI2, 6MI3, 6Nn30, 6Pt2, 6Ps7; Teacher's Resource 17.1, 17.2

43

Handling data

Remember

A **ready reckoner** is a table used to convert between two different scales or measures. You need to understand ratio to make and use a ready reckoner.

Line graphs are used to present **continuous data**. Any point on the line represents meaningful data.

A **pie chart** is used to compare **categorical data**. You need to understand and calculate **percentages** to extract the data in a pie chart.

You will need:
ruler

Vocabulary
origin,
line graph,
ready reckoner,
pie chart

1   Metres and yards are used as units to describe the distance to nearby places.

Make a ready reckoner for metres and yards.

metres	yards
1	1.0912
100	
200	
500	
1000	
2000	
5000	
10000	

yards	metres
1	0.9091
100	
200	
500	
1000	
2000	
5000	
10000	

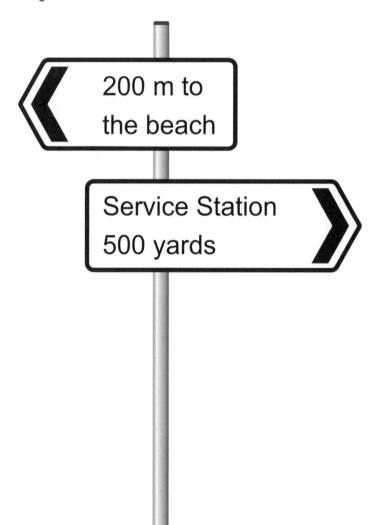

200 m to the beach

Service Station 500 yards

Hint: Use doubling and multiplying by 5 to complete the ready reckoners.

Unit 2C: Handling data and problem solving
CPM framework 6Dh1, 6Pt2, 6Ps8; Teacher's Resource 20.1, 20.2

2 Create a line graph for converting between metres and yards.

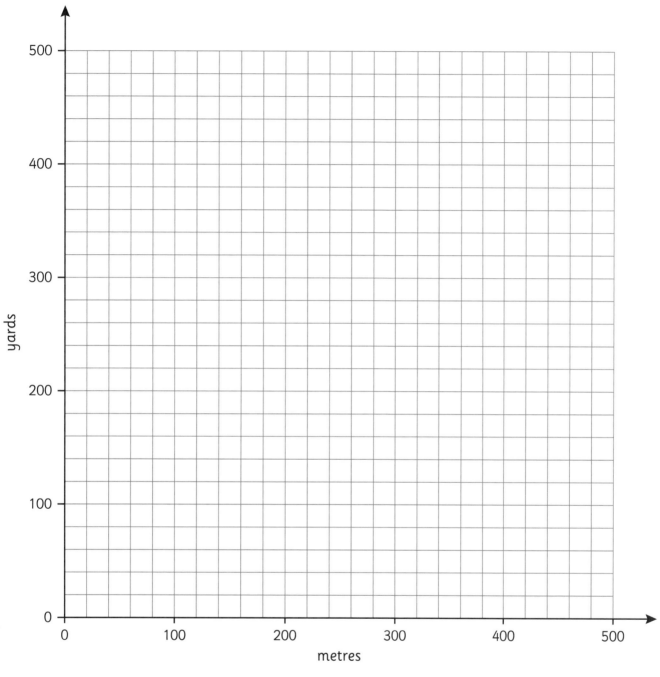

yards

metres

Use the line graph to convert 275 yards to metres.

275 yards = approximately ☐ metres

Use the line graph to convert 320 metres to yards.

320 metres = approximately ☐ yards

Hint: Plot about three points from the ready reckoner on the graph and draw a straight line through them to the origin (0, 0).

3 250 people were asked to respond to this survey.
This is the pie chart made from the data collected.

Are the school holidays too short?

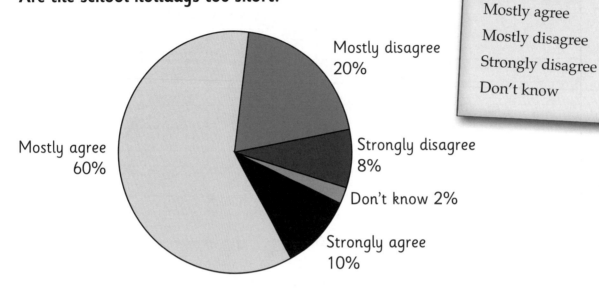

Mostly disagree
20%

Strongly disagree
8%

Don't know 2%

Strongly agree
10%

Mostly agree
60%

The school holidays are too short.
Do you agree?

Strongly agree ☐
Mostly agree ☐
Mostly disagree ☐
Strongly disagree ☐
Don't know ☐

Convert the data from the pie chart into a bar graph.

Use this space for your working.

Unit 2C: Handling data and problem solving
CPM framework 6Dh1, 6Pt2, 6Ps8; Teacher's Resource 20.1, 20.2

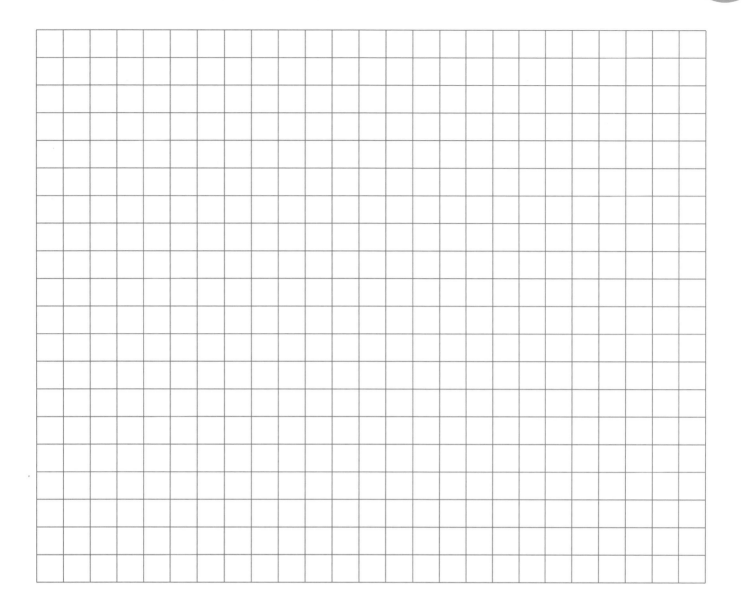

Use the data from the pie chart or your bar graph to write three true statements.

1 _____

2 _____

3 _____

Hint: Try working out how many people are represented by 10% and 1% first.
Draw a table of the data before planning the scale of the graph.

Probability and averages

You will need: calculator (optional), coloured pens or pencils

Remember

The **mode**, **median** and **mean** are three types of **average** for a set of data.

Probability is the chance of a particular outcome occurring. You can use words such as **impossible** or **likely** to describe probability.

You can also use proportion, fractions or percentages, for example:
* there is a one in four chance
* there is a 25% chance.

Vocabulary

average, mode, mean, median, range, probability, likelihood, chance, likely, unlikely, impossible, equally likely, certain

1   11 people are in a queue. These are the heights of the people.

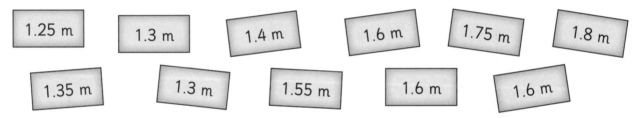

What is the chance that the first person in the queue is taller than 1.3 m? Why?

What is the chance that the first person is shorter than 1.2 m? Why?

Unit 2C: Handling data and problem solving, **Unit 3A:** Number and problem solving
CPM framework 6Dh2, 6Dh3, 6Db1; Teacher's Resource 21.1, 22.1

What is the range of heights? ☐

What is the modal height? ☐

What is the median height? ☐

What is the mean height? ☐

> **Hint:** Start by writing the data in order from shortest to tallest. If using a calculator to work out the mean, be careful to enter the data correctly.

2 You have to spin a 6 to start a game. You can choose any of these spinners.

Which spinner has the greatest chance of spinning a 6?

☐

Describe the probability of spinning a 6 on this spinner.

A — hexagon spinner with 6, 1, 2, 5, 4, 3

B — square spinner with 0, 6, 2, 4

C — pentagon spinner with 6, 3, 6, 4, 5

D — hexagon spinner with 6, 2, 4, 4, 6, 2

E — pentagon spinner with 5, 1, 4, 2, 3

F — square spinner with 1, 6, 6, 1

Which spinner has the least chance of spinning a 6? ☐

Describe the probability of spinning a 6 on this spinner.

Write the spinner letters in order, from the greatest to the least chance of spinning a 6.

☐ , ☐ , ☐ , ☐ , ☐ , ☐

> **Hint:** Look at what fraction of each spinner will give a score of 6.

Unit 2C: Handling data and problem solving, **Unit 3A:** Number and problem solving
CPM framework 6Dh2, 6Dh3, 6Db1; Teacher's Resource 21.1, 22.1

49

3 Colour the balls in the bag so that all of these statements are true.

- There is a 1 in 5 chance of taking a red ball.
- It is impossible to take a blue ball.
- There is a 1 in 4 chance of taking a yellow ball.
- It is unlikely that a green ball will be taken.
- There is an even chance of taking a purple ball.

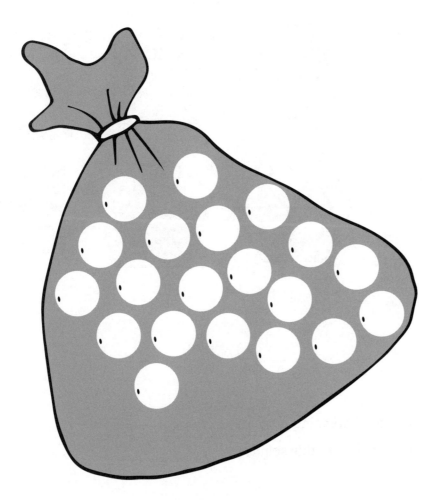

Add four more coloured balls to the bag to make **all** of the statements **untrue**.

> **Hint:** Check each of the statements against the contents of the bag.

Unit 2C: Handling data and problem solving, **Unit 3A:** Number and problem solving
CPM framework 6Dh2, 6Dh3, 6Db1; Teacher's Resource 21.1, 22.1

Fractions

Remember

You can simplify a fraction by finding **equivalent fractions**.
Divide the **numerator** and the **denominator** by a
common factor to find an equivalent fraction. When there are
no more common factors the fraction is in its **simplest form**.

Improper fractions and **mixed numbers** are two ways of
writing fractions greater than 1.

For example, $\frac{3}{2} = 1\frac{1}{2}$.

Vocabulary

equivalent fraction,
simplify, cancel,
improper fraction,
mixed number

1 Match each of the numbers in the circles to its simplified form in the rectangles.

$\frac{8}{16}$ $\frac{32}{40}$ $\frac{21}{28}$ $\frac{20}{80}$

$\frac{6}{30}$ $\frac{6}{60}$ $\frac{70}{100}$

$\frac{1}{2}$ $\frac{3}{4}$ $\frac{4}{5}$ $\frac{3}{10}$

$\frac{1}{4}$ $\frac{1}{5}$ $\frac{1}{10}$ $\frac{7}{10}$

$\frac{20}{100}$ $\frac{9}{30}$ $\frac{27}{90}$ $\frac{17}{34}$ $\frac{75}{100}$

$\frac{5}{20}$ $\frac{28}{40}$ $\frac{40}{50}$ $\frac{11}{110}$

2 Start at A, B, C or D. If the fraction is greater than $\frac{3}{4}$ take the right arrow, if it is less than $\frac{3}{4}$ take the left.

Which player gets to the goal?

	A		B		C		D	
← $\frac{1}{8}$ →	↑	← $\frac{9}{24}$ →	**Goal**			← $\frac{19}{28}$ →	↑	← $\frac{93}{100}$ →
↑	← $\frac{13}{16}$ →	↑	← $\frac{7}{12}$ →		← $\frac{18}{23}$ →	↑	← $\frac{21}{32}$ →	↑
← $\frac{3}{16}$ →	↑	← $\frac{71}{100}$ →	↑	← $\frac{9}{40}$ →	↑	← $\frac{11}{16}$ →	↑	← $\frac{7}{8}$ →
↑	← $\frac{1}{12}$ →	↑	← $\frac{23}{40}$ →	↑	← $\frac{17}{20}$ →	↑	← $\frac{23}{28}$ →	↑
← $\frac{9}{32}$ →	↑	← $\frac{19}{24}$ →	↑	← $\frac{10}{12}$ →	↑	← $\frac{9}{24}$ →	↑	← $\frac{12}{20}$ →
↑	← $\frac{15}{16}$ →	↑	← $\frac{1}{2}$ →	↑	← $\frac{73}{100}$ →	↑	← $\frac{77}{100}$ →	↑
← $\frac{7}{8}$ →	↑	← $\frac{3}{8}$ →	↑	← $\frac{5}{24}$ →	↑	← $\frac{5}{8}$ →	↑	← $\frac{15}{24}$ →
↑	← $\frac{17}{28}$ →	↑	← $\frac{29}{40}$ →	↑	← $\frac{13}{16}$ →	↑	← $\frac{34}{40}$ →	↑
← $\frac{21}{24}$ →	↑	← $\frac{7}{12}$ →	↑	← $\frac{19}{28}$ →	↑	← $\frac{29}{40}$ →	↑	← $\frac{9}{16}$ →
↑	← $\frac{27}{40}$ →	↑	← $\frac{33}{40}$ →	↑	← $\frac{7}{8}$ →	↑	← $\frac{11}{12}$ →	↑
	A		**B**		**C**		**D**	

3 Write four mixed numbers between $4\frac{1}{4}$ and $4\frac{1}{2}$.

Mark $4\frac{1}{4}$ and $4\frac{1}{2}$ on the number line.

4   5

Mark the four mixed numbers on the number line, in order.

Unit 3A: Number and problem solving
CPM framework 6Nn21, 6Nn22, 6Nn24, 6Nn25, 6Nn26; Teacher's Resource 27.1, 27.2

Decimals and percentages

Remember

To solve these problems you need to understand that $1\% = \frac{1}{100}$.

You can draw a number line to help order and compare **numbers**, **fractions**, **decimals** and **percentages**.

You will need:
a calculator,
1–10 number cards

Vocabulary
fraction, decimal, percentage

1 Draw a line from each fraction to the equivalent percentage.

50%	25%	10%	100%	20%

7%	90%	31%	30%	77%

$\frac{1}{10}$	$\frac{1}{2}$	$\frac{7}{100}$	$\frac{1}{4}$	$\frac{9}{10}$

1	$\frac{31}{100}$	$\frac{1}{5}$	$\frac{3}{10}$	$\frac{77}{100}$

2 There are five identical laptops for sale. Which is the cheapest?

A Special offer – Was $542, now 30% off!

B Special offer – Was $759.90, now $\frac{1}{2}$ price!

C Special offer – Was $508, now 25% off!

D Special offer – Was $570.42, now $\frac{1}{3}$ off!

E Special offer – Was $474, now 20% off!

Hint: To work out the percentage of a price, first work out 10%.

3 Use a calculator or mental recall to convert each of these fractions to a decimal. Write both the fraction and the decimal on the number line.

$\frac{9}{20}$ $\frac{53}{100}$ $\frac{24}{50}$ $\frac{13}{25}$ $\frac{3}{5}$

_____ _____ _____ _____ _____

0.3 ←————————————————————————————————→ 0.7

Hint: Look at the fraction first to check whether to use the calculator or if it is a known fact.

4 Find some fractions that will fit between $\frac{3}{4}$ and $\frac{4}{5}$ on the number line.

0 ————— $\frac{1}{4}$ ————— $\frac{1}{2}$ ————— $\frac{3}{4}$ ————— 1

Hint: Try converting the fractions to decimals.
Find decimals that can easily be converted to fractions that are between $\frac{3}{4}$ and $\frac{4}{5}$.
Simplify fractions if possible.

5 This is a game for two players.

Shuffle a set of 1–10 number cards.

Take two number cards. Position one above the other to make a fraction.

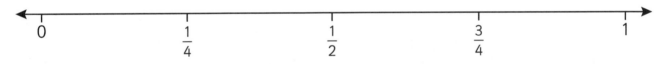

Example: Take 3 and 4 and make $\frac{3}{4}$.

Both players write down another fraction that is as close as possible to the fraction made by the cards, but without exceeding it.

The players reveal their fractions. The player whose fraction is closer keeps the cards.

Continue playing until all of the cards are gone. The player with the most cards is the winner.

Hint: Check who is closer by converting the fractions to decimals.

Unit 3A: Number and problem solving
CPM framework 6Nn23, 6Nn28, 6Nn29, 6Ps8; Teacher's Resource 28.1, 28.2

Ratio and proportion

Remember

Use **proportion** to describe the size of one part compared to the whole, for example, 'In every packet of 12 sweets, three are orange,' or '$\frac{1}{4}$ of the sweets are orange.'

Use **ratio** to describe the size of one part compared to another part, for example, 'For every nine red sweets there are three orange sweets,' or 'for every three red sweets there is one orange sweet,' or 'the ratio of red sweets to orange sweets is 3 : 1.'

Vocabulary

ratio, proportion, direct proportion

1   By only colouring the small, whole squares, which of these square grids can you colour in the ratio 1 : 3?

Describe what you have found. Explain the pattern.

2 Cheng is catering for a banquet.

This is a recipe for pancakes.

Cheng tried to use direct proportion to work out the ingredients needed for more pancakes.

This is his new recipe.

> **Pancakes**
> *Makes 12 pancakes.*
>
> 140 g flour
> 2 eggs
> 240 ml milk

> To make more pancakes.
> 150 g flour, 12 eggs,
> 250 ml milk

What mistakes has Cheng made?

There will be 126 guests.

Rewrite the recipe with the quantities needed so that each guest will have one pancake.

Hint: Try partitioning 126 into numbers of guests that are easier to work out with a recipe for 12.
Use a table like this:

Number of pancakes	Flour (g)	Eggs	Milk (ml)
12	140	2	240
?	?	?	?

3 Anil bought some pet fish to start his aquarium. He spent $40.

Some of the fish are guppies. They cost $3.60 each.

Some of the fish are mollies. They cost $2.80 each.

What proportion of the fish are guppies?

What proportion of the fish are mollies?

What is the ratio in the tank of guppies to mollies?

Hint: First find a number of mollies and guppies that would cost a total of $40.

Unit 3A: Number and problem solving
CPM framework 6Nn30, 6Ps7; Teacher's Resource 29.1

Metric and imperial measures

You will need:
calculator (optional)

Remember

These are some equivalent quantities in **imperial units** of measurement:

1 imperial **pint** = 20 imperial **fluid ounces**
1 imperial **pound** = 16 **imperial ounces**
1 imperial **foot** = 12 **imperial inches**

You should know what common imperial units are used to measure length, mass and volume.

Vocabulary
miles, feet, inches, gallon, quart, pint, pounds, ounces

1 Label divisions on the measuring jug so that it can be used to measure liquid in both imperial pints and litres.

There are 20 fluid ounces (fl. oz) in one imperial pint.

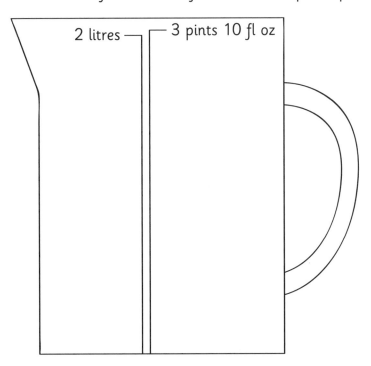

2 litres — ┌─ 3 pints 10 fl oz

Use your measuring jug scales to convert these measurements.

1 litre = approximately ☐ pint(s) and ☐ fl. oz

200ml = approximately ☐ pint(s) and ☐ fl. oz

15 fl. oz = approximately ☐ ml

2 pints and 5 fl. oz = approximately ☐ litres

Hint: Measure and divide up each scale separately. Check that points that should be approximately equal on the two scales line up, for example, 1 pint equals approximately 570 ml (rounded to the nearest 10 ml).

Unit 3B: Measure and problem solving
CPM framework 6MI1, 6MI2, 6MI3, 6MI5, 6Pt2, 6Ps3; Teacher's Resource 30.1, 30.2

57

2   A nurse asked six people to tell her their heights.
They all wrote them on sticky notes and gave them to her.

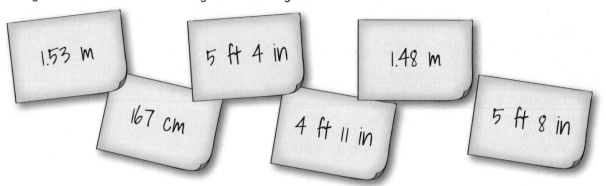

The nurse dropped her folder and the sticky notes got muddled.

Use the clues to write the correct height next to each name in the table below.

Clues

Eman is not the shortest or tallest.

Anton is approximately 1 inch taller than Lily.

Bashir is taller than Musa, but shorter than Eman.

Lily is the closest in height to 150cm.

> **Hint:** Convert all the measurements so that they are in the same units.

Name	Height
Anton	
Bashir	
Eman	
Lily	
Musa	
Salma	

Use this space for your working.

Unit 3B: Measure and problem solving
CPM framework 6MI1, 6MI2, 6MI3, 6MI5, 6Pt2, 6Ps3; Teacher's Resource 30.1, 30.2

3 Convert this recipe into metric measures for 20 people.

1 oz = approximately 28 g

Onion, cheese and olive tart
Serves 8 people

2 oz butter
4 large onions
4 tbsp muscovado sugar
4 tbsp balsamic vinegar
2 lb puff pastry
8 oz feta cheese
12 oz black olives
2 tbsp olive oil

Hint: Try working out the quantities for 20 people in imperial measures first, then convert the recipe to metric.

Unit 3B: Measure and problem solving
CPM framework 6MI1, 6MI2, 6MI3, 6MI5, 6Pt2, 6Ps3; Teacher's Resource 30.1, 30.2

59

Time zones

Vocabulary

time zone, universal time

Remember

To solve these problems you need to understand that time is different in different **zones** around the world.

You can draw a time line and use it like a number line to work out **time intervals**.

1   Complete this table to show the time differences between cities.

Taipei
Sunday pm

New Delhi
Sunday pm

Reykjavik
Sunday am

Adelaide
Sunday pm

Bogota
Sunday am

Nairobi
Sunday pm

Kathmandu
Sunday pm

Kiribati
Monday am

Taipei							
	New Delhi						
		Reykjavik					
			Adelaide				
				Bogota			
					Nairobi		
						Kathmandu	
							Kiribati

Unit 2B: Measure and problem solving, **Unit 3B:** Measure and problem solving
CPM framework 6Mt1, 6Mt2, 6Mt3, 6Mt4, 6Mt5, 6Mt8, 6Pt2, 6Ps2; Teacher's Resource 18.2, 31.1

2   Use the table and clocks from question 1 to solve these problems.

If it is 08:45 on Monday 3rd August 2020 in Adelaide, what time and date is it in Reykjavik?

If it is 17:32 on Wednesday 28th February 2024 in Bogota, what is the time and date in Nairobi?

If it is 07:05 on Tuesday 1st January 2019 in Kiribati, what is the time and date in New Delhi?

Hint: Remember to check which time is ahead and which time is behind.

3   Rosa, Mira and Alma are solving a puzzle. They all start the puzzle when it is 14:38 in Rosa's country. The time in Mira's country is 4 hours ahead of the time in Rosa's. The time in Alma's country is 7 hours behind the time in Rosa's.

These are the times on each person's clock when they finished.

Rosa's clock    Mira's clock    Alma's clock

How long did each person take to complete the puzzle?

This is Lulu.

She finished the puzzle at the time shown on her clock. She was not the first or last to finish.

What might be the time difference between her and Rosa?

_____

Hint: Draw a time line and map each person's local start and finish times.

Unit 2B: Measure and problem solving, **Unit 3B:** Measure and problem solving
CPM framework 6Mt1, 6Mt2, 6Mt3, 6Mt4, 6Mt5, 6Mt8, 6Pt2, 6Ps2; Teacher's Resource 18.2, 31.1

61

Area and perimeter

Remember
Perimeter is measured in units of length, for example, cm or m.
Area is measured in square units, for example, cm² or m².

Vocabulary
formula

1 Explain the formula for calculating the area of a rectangle.

Hint: Draw and use an example to support the explanation.

2 Without measuring, calculate the perimeter of each shape.

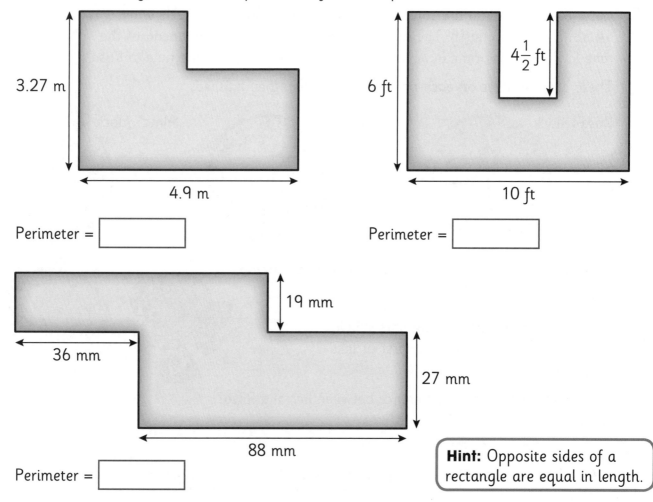

3.27 m

4.9 m

Perimeter = [ ]

6 ft

$4\frac{1}{2}$ ft

10 ft

Perimeter = [ ]

36 mm

19 mm

27 mm

88 mm

Perimeter = [ ]

Hint: Opposite sides of a rectangle are equal in length.

Unit 2B: Measure and problem solving, **Unit 3B:** Measure and problem solving
CPM framework 6Ma1, 6Ma2, 6Ma3, 6Pt2, 6Pt4; Teacher's Resource 19.1, 32.1, 32.2

3 The area of each square of this grid is 1 cm². It is 10 squares wide and 10 squares long.

Estimate what area of the grid is shaded. ☐

Use counting to find out approximately what area of this grid is shaded. ☐

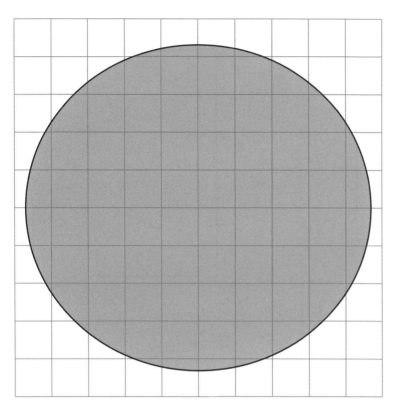

4 A floor of wooden tiles is laid with this pattern.
All of the tiles are the same size.

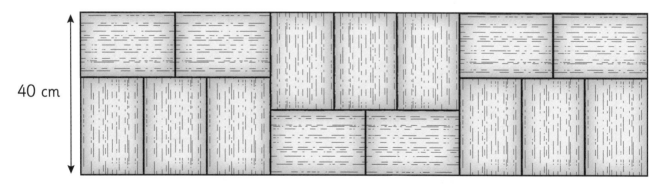

40 cm

Work out the area and perimeter of one tile.

Area = ☐   Perimeter = ☐

Hint: Look at the ratio of the short side to the long side of each tile.
Work out the length of each side.

Unit 2B: Measure and problem solving, **Unit 3B:** Measure and problem solving
CPM framework 6Ma1, 6Ma2, 6Ma3, 6Pt2, 6Pt4; Teacher's Resource 19.1, 32.1, 32.2

63

5 Each of these rectangles is made up of an outer and inner area.

For each rectangle, colour the part of the rectangle that has the larger area red and the smaller area blue.

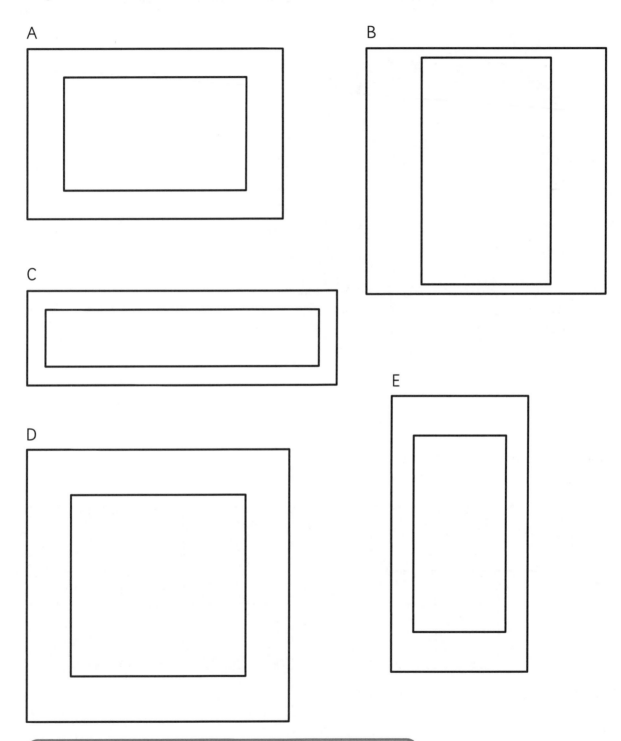

A

B

C

E

D

> **Hint:** Measure the sides of the rectangles to work out their area. Subtract the inner rectangle from the outer rectangle to find the area of the outer area.

Unit 2B: Measure and problem solving, Unit 3B: Measure and problem solving
CPM framework 6Ma1, 6Ma2, 6Ma3, 6Pt2, 6Pt4; Teacher's Resource 19.1, 32.1, 32.2

3D shapes

Remember

Pyramids and prisms are types of **polyhedra**.
A polyhedron is a closed 3D shape with flat **faces**.
The faces meet at **edges**. The edges meet at **vertices**.

A polyhedron with all its faces the same shape and size
is **regular**.

You will need: ruler, protractor

Vocabulary

pyramid, prism, octahedron

1   Each of these diagrams is an incomplete net of a closed 3D shape.

In each of them, one face is missing.

Draw the missing face as accurately as you can.
Use a ruler and protractor.

Then complete the information about
each net.

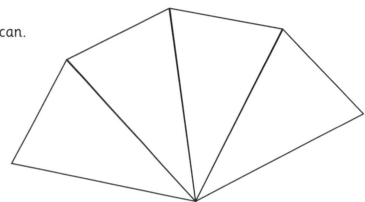

Number of faces: ☐

Number of edges: ☐

Number of vertices: ☐

Name of shape: ☐

Number of faces: ☐

Number of edges: ☐

Number of vertices: ☐

Name of shape: ☐

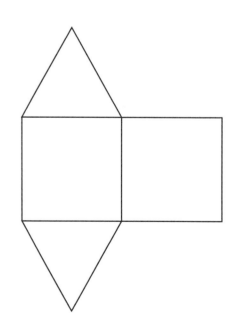

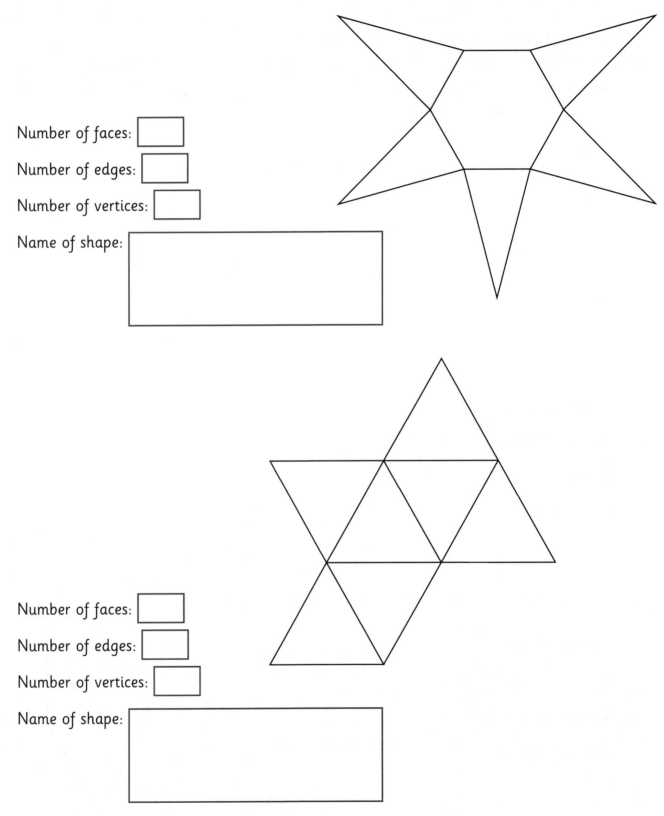

Number of faces: ☐

Number of edges: ☐

Number of vertices: ☐

Name of shape: ☐

Number of faces: ☐

Number of edges: ☐

Number of vertices: ☐

Name of shape: ☐

Copy the shapes onto card and make the 3D shapes to check your answers.

Unit 3C: Geometry and problem solving,
CPM framework 6Gs2, 6Gs4, 6Pt4; Teacher's Resource 33.1, 33.2

2 This is a rectangle-based pyramid. The base is not a square.

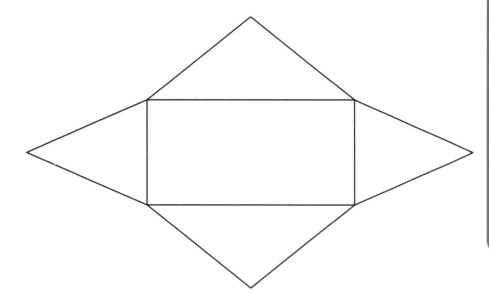

Hint: Notice that the triangles are not all the same. They are all isosceles and opposite pairs are the same shape and size. Use trial and improvement to change the sizes of the triangles until they fit together to make a rectangle-based pyramid.

Copy the net onto card and make the pyramid.

Try to make your own net of a rectangle-based pyramid below.

Choose your own size rectangular base, different from the one above.

2D shapes and transformations

You will need: ruler

Remember

To solve these problems you need to know the properties of different 2D shapes.

A quadrilateral is a closed 2D shape. It has four straight sides and four vertices.

Vocabulary

parallelogram, rhombus, trapezium, polygon

1   On each of these four quadrant grids, the line is one side of a quadrilateral. Draw the quadrilateral.

Each quadrilateral has four vertices. Two of the vertices are not on the original line. Write these two coordinates under each quadrilateral.

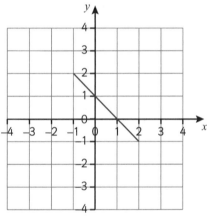

A square

(⬚ , ⬚), (⬚ , ⬚)

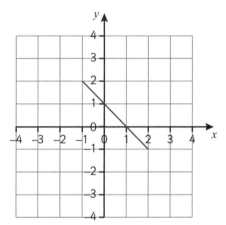

A trapezium

(⬚ , ⬚), (⬚ , ⬚)

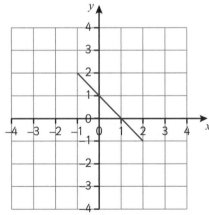

A parallelogram with no right angles

(⬚ , ⬚), (⬚ , ⬚)

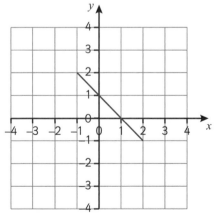

A kite

(⬚ , ⬚), (⬚ , ⬚)

Unit 3C: Geometry and problem solving
CPM framework 6Gs1, 6Gs3, 6Gp1, 6Gp2, 6Pt4; Teacher's Resource 35.1

2 On the grid, draw a rectangle with vertices (−1, 5), (−2, 6), (−4, 2), (−5, 3).

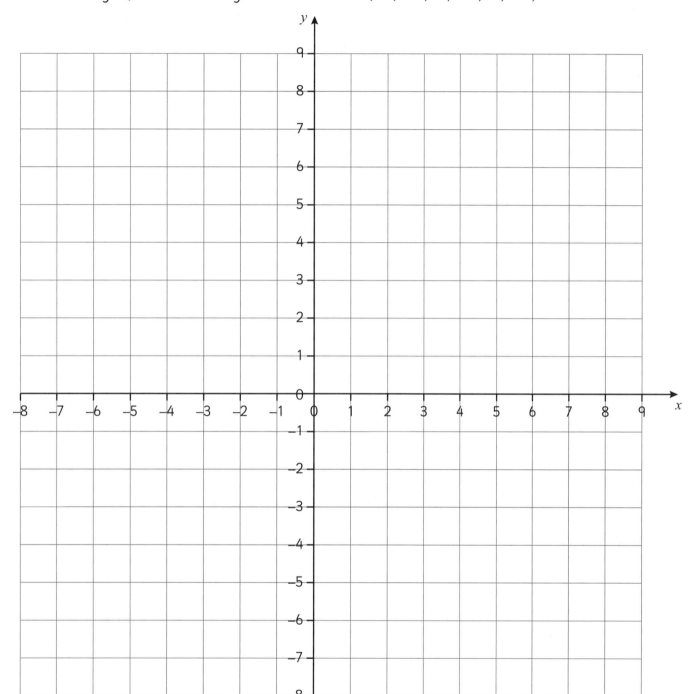

Translate the rectangle by −1 on the *x*-axis and −3 on the *y*-axis.

Shade in both rectangles together to make an octagon.

Rotate the octagon 90° clockwise about (−5, −1).

Draw a line through all the points where the *x*-coordinate is 1.

Reflect the two octagons over the line.

What are the coordinates of the vertices of the octagon
that lie completely in the bottom right quadrant? _____

Angles

Remember
The **angles of a triangle** add up to 180°.
The **angles along a straight line** add up to 180°.
The **angles around a point** add up to 360°.

You will need: protractor, ruler

1   Find and mark the points that are halfway along the sides of the triangle.

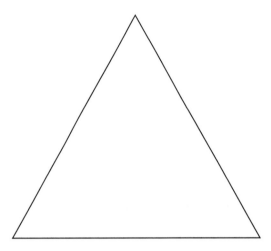

Join the three marks with straight lines to form a triangle.

Measure and label the angles of the larger and smaller triangles.

Do the same with this triangle.   Now do the same with this triangle.

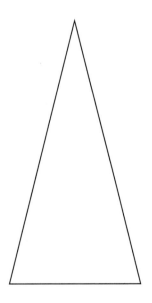
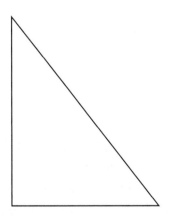

Unit 3C: Geometry and problem solving
CPM framework 6Gs5, 6Gs6, 6Pt4; Teacher's Resource 35.1

Investigate by drawing some triangles of your own.

Describe what you have discovered.

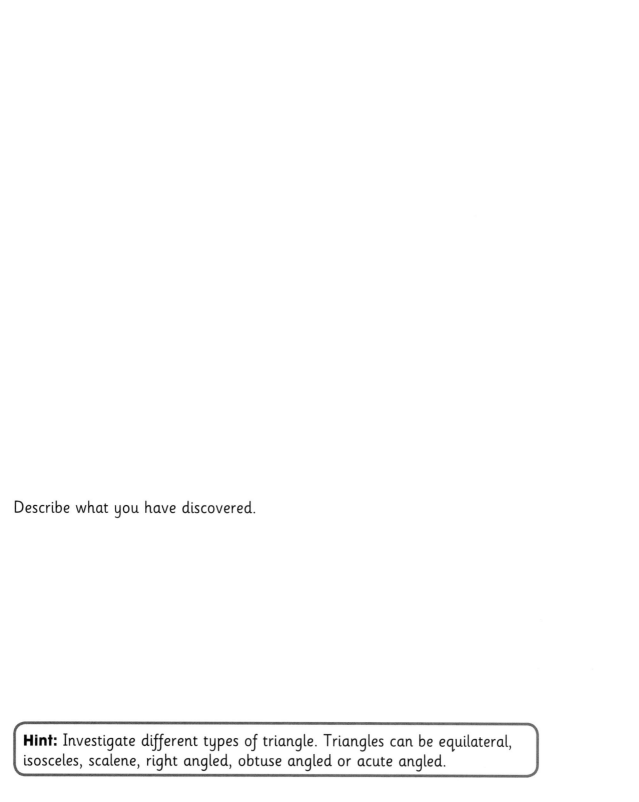

> **Hint:** Investigate different types of triangle. Triangles can be equilateral, isosceles, scalene, right angled, obtuse angled or acute angled.

2 Draw a quadrilateral in which all the angles are different sizes.
Label the angles.

Draw a quadrilateral in which two of the angles are the same size.
Label the angles.

Draw a quadrilateral in which three of the angles are the same
size. Label the angles.

Draw a quadrilateral where all four angles are the same size.
Label the angles.

Investigate the sum of the angles in quadrilaterals.

Describe what you find out.

Unit 3C: Geometry and problem solving
CPM framework 6Gs5, 6Gs6, 6Pt4; Teacher's Resource 35.1

Problems and puzzles

You will need: a ruler, 2 sets of 1–10 number cards, 10 envelopes

Remember

Use ordered lists and tables to help you solve problems systematically.

To solve problems with logical reasoning use sentences such as: 'If this is true, then that must also be true,' or 'If this is true, then that must not be true.'

Vocabulary

logical reasoning, systematically, generalised statement

1   If the shaded squares on this grid were reflected over both mirror lines, how many unshaded squares would be left?

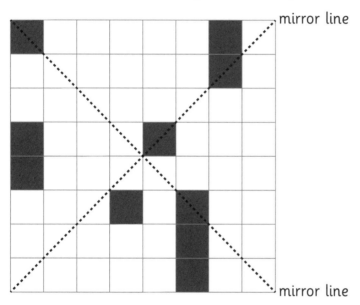

mirror line

mirror line

Hint: Reflect all the shaded squares over one mirror line first, then reflect them over the other line. The finished design should have two lines of symmetry.

2

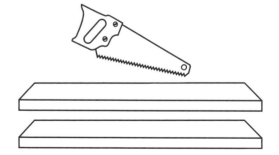

I had two planks of wood the same length. I cut one of the planks. One of the pieces is now the mean average of the other two.

Investigate and explain how the plank of wood was cut.

3 This is an irregular dodecagon.
It has 12 sides that are all the same length.

What is the greatest number of pieces the
shape can be cut into, with two straight lines?

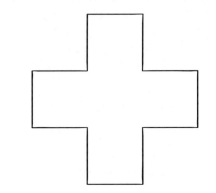

Use these shapes to try different cuts.

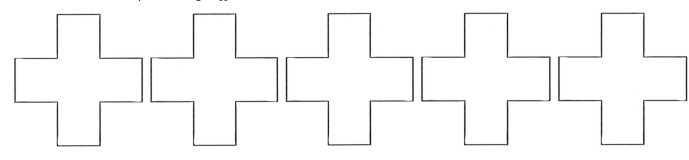

Hint: More than four pieces can be made.

4 Use the digit 8 eight times, with any combination of addition,
subtraction, multiplication and division, to make 1000.

Example: $(88 + 8 + 8 - 8 - 8 - 8) \times 8 = 640$ ✗   Not 1000

Use this space to record your calculations.

CPM Framework 6Ps2, 6Ps3, 6Ps4, 6Ps5

5 Complete this activity with a partner.

Each person needs a set of 1–10 number cards and 5 envelopes.

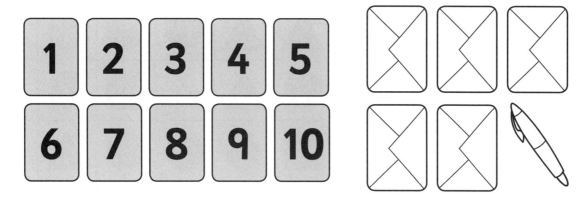

Secretly, put two cards into each envelope and write the total of the two cards on the envelope.

Swap your set of envelopes with those of your partner.

Work systematically to try to work out what pairs of number cards your partner has put together.

> **Hint:** It will not always be possible to work out which cards are in which envelopes. Work systematically to find out what combinations there could be in each envelope, then use logical reasoning to work out which pairs of cards make up the whole set.

6 Each shape in the grid represents a single-digit number.

Work out the missing totals and which shape is missing from the grid.

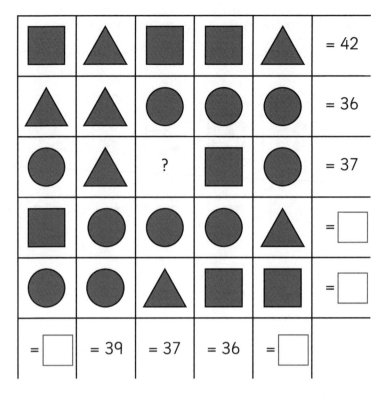

Hint: Start by trying different numbers for the triangle and circle that make the second column and second row true. Use logical reasoning to work out whether the triangle or circle represents a greater number and what the difference between those numbers must be.

7 Parveen planted a fruit tree. Each year she recorded how many fruits it had produced.

Year	1	2	3	4	5
Number of fruits	1	4	7	10	13

(a) If the pattern of fruits continues, how many fruits will there be in the 9th year? _____

(b) Describe the relationship between the year number and the number of fruits in that year.

_____

(c) Use the relationship to complete this table.

Year	8	10	20	50	100
Number of fruits					

(d) If the pattern continues, in which year will there be 400 fruits? _____

CPM Framework 6Ps2, 6Ps3, 6Ps4, 6Ps5

8 Four children entered a puzzle competition. They each belong to a different mathematics club. They each wore a number from 1 to 4.

Use the clues to complete the information about the competition results.

Clues

- Jasem came first.
- The competitor wearing number 2 came from the 'Numberfuns' club.
- Tomas was not from the 'Geometers' club.
- The 4th place competitor was from the 'Calculots' club.
- Eman wore number 1.
- Maria achieved a higher place than Eman.
- The person who came second wore number 3.
- The competitor from 'Geometers' was higher placed than the competitor from the 'Dataist' club.
- Only one of the competitors wore the same number as their final position.

Hint: Start by working out which number should be written on each trophy. Use logical reasoning to work out which numbers each could and could not be.

Resource 1
Place-value chart

900000	90000	9000	900	90	9	0.9	0.09
800000	80000	8000	800	80	8	0.8	0.08
700000	70000	7000	700	70	7	0.7	0.07
600000	60000	6000	600	60	6	0.6	0.06
500000	50000	5000	500	50	5	0.5	0.05
400000	40000	4000	400	40	4	0.4	0.04
300000	30000	3000	300	30	3	0.3	0.03
200000	20000	2000	200	20	2	0.2	0.02
100000	10000	1000	100	10	1	0.1	0.01

Photocopiable resources

Resource 2
Nets

Cut out these nets carefully.
Fold each one to make a 3D shape.

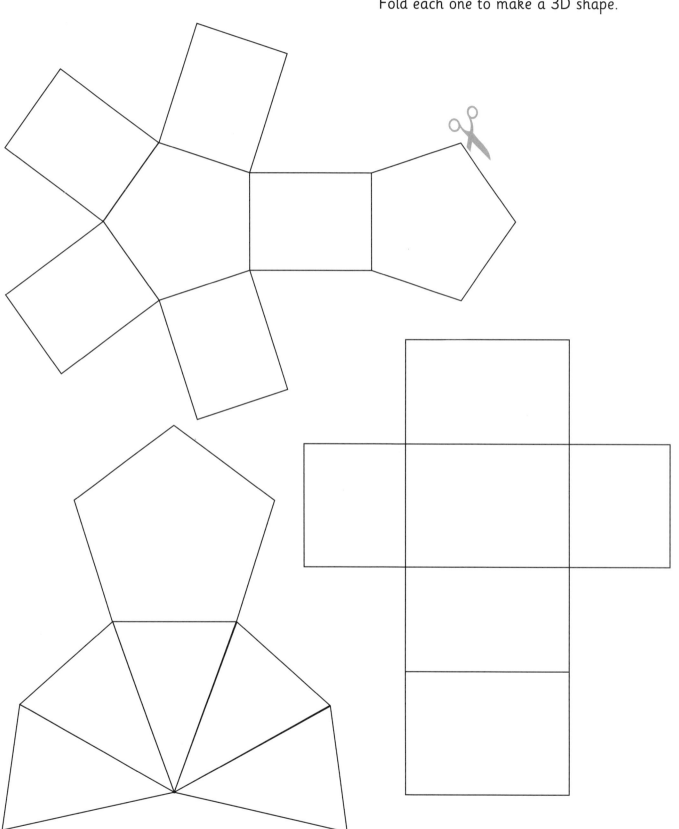

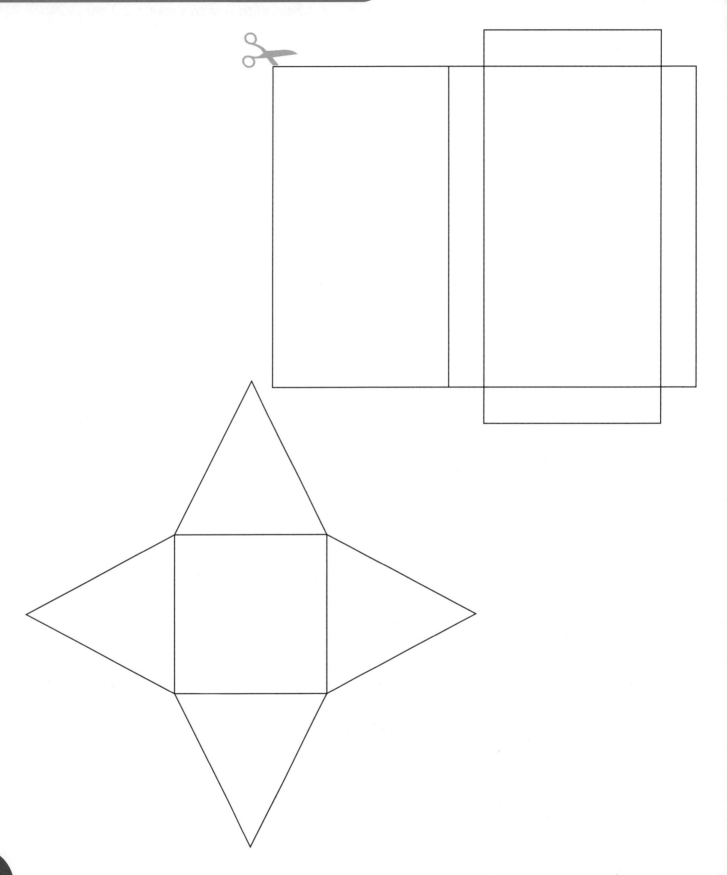

Photocopiable resources

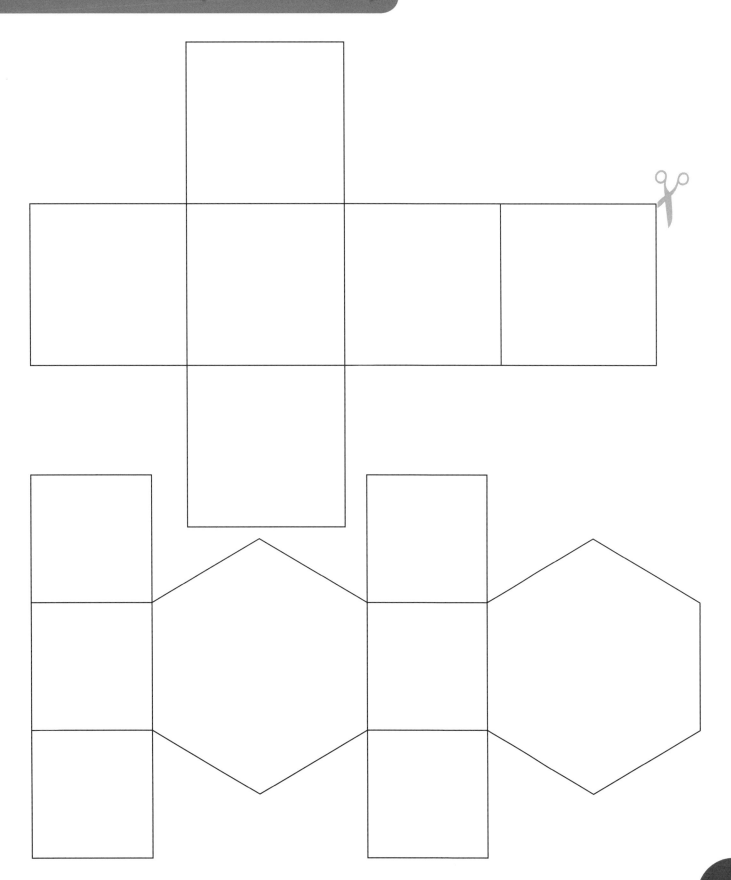

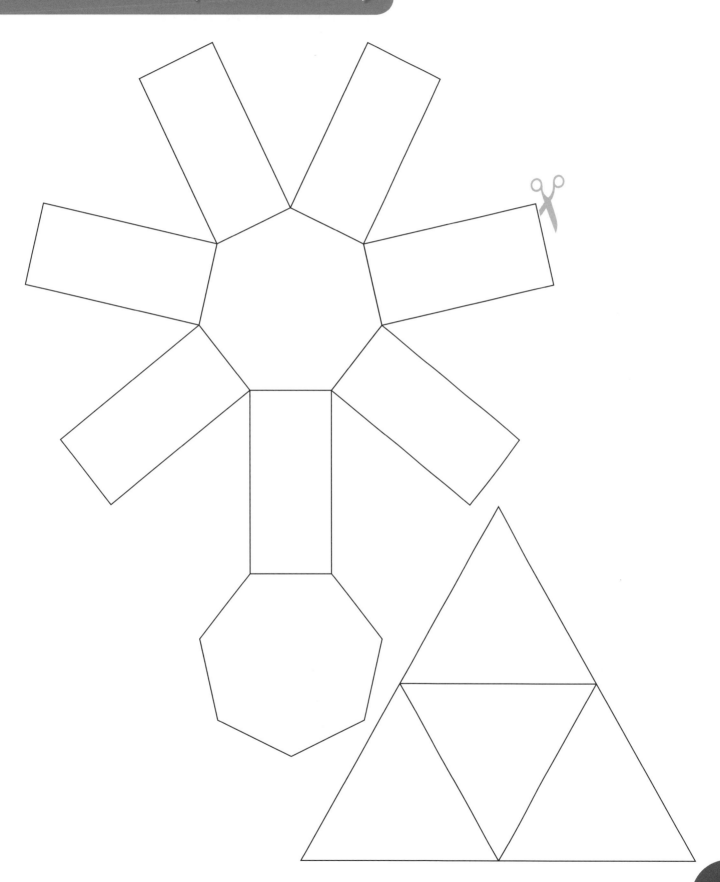

Answers

Page 4 The number system

1 The hidden number is 'six'.

2
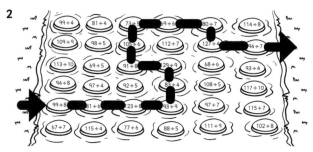

Number line showing:
0, 1085, 2458, 5230, 7312, 9103, 10000 with 9862 marked.

3 986 577 > 985 677

9.23 + 8.69 > 27.74 − 9.95

8.45 × 100 < 845 000 ÷ 100

5 × 210 = 150 × 7

8.29 < 8.3

4 A good approximation would be around 200 000 ml / 200 litres. This is 12500 × 16.

The actual capacity is 199 616 ml / 199.616 litres

Page 6 Multiples, factors and primes

1 5

35, 70, 105, 140, 175

2 Prime numbers: 83, 89, 97

Which numbers in this grid have the most factors? 84, 90 and 96 all have 12 factors.

81 and 100 have an odd number of factors because they are square numbers.

3 The correct exit is J.

Example explanation:

Even number + even number = even number (turn right)

Odd number × even number = even number (turn right)

Odd number − odd number = even number (turn right)

Odd number × odd number = odd number (turn left)

Even number × even number = even number (turn right)

Odd number − even number = odd number (turn left)

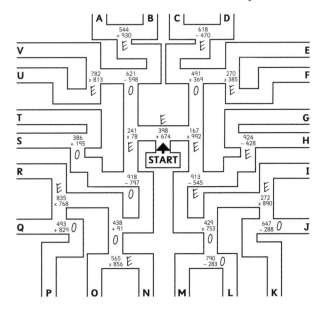

4 5, 8, 12, 18, 24, 30, 36

One possible observation:

All, except the first sum, are even.

Page 9 Multiplication and division (1)

1 number ÷10 = number × 100 ÷1000

number ×10 ÷1000 = number ÷1000 × 10

number ×100 = number ×10 ×10

number ×10 ×100 = number ×10 ×10 ×10

number × 100 ÷ 10 = number ÷ 100 × 1000

2

A grid of division puzzles with a path marked.

3 Game

4 48 × 51 = 2448. This is the closest to 2500.

Page 13 Number sequences

1 Learner's own sequence; 2 decimal places

Learner's own sequence; 11th term

2 −0.5, 0.25, 1, 1.75, 2.5

+0.75

6.25

3 $11\frac{1}{4}$, $11\frac{5}{8}$, 12, $12\frac{3}{8}$, $12\frac{6}{8}$ (or $12\frac{3}{4}$), $13\frac{1}{8}$

$+\frac{3}{8}$

$14\frac{5}{8}$

4 20, 30, 45, 67.5, 101.25

200, 300, 450, 675, 1012.5

10, 15, 22.5, 33.75, 50.625

7.2, 10.8, 16.2, 24.3, 36.45

Page 15 Length

1 Check that the 1st two sides drawn are 7.3 cm and 4.6 cm

The third side of the triangle should be 86 mm to the nearest mm.

2 The sides of the isosceles right angled triangles should be:

6.5 cm, 6.5 cm, 9.2 cm

4.6 cm, 4.6 cm, 6. 5cm

3 27.9 cm, 982.5 m, 98 250 cm

4 22 cm

5 The learner should find that the circumference is approximately 3 times larger than the widest distance across the circle, and that the circumference is a bit more than 3 times.

Page 18 Timetables and calendars

1. 8th July or 8th December
2. 23rd March (on a leap year)
3. **a)** Sunday
   b) Tuesday
   c) Saturday
   d) Tuesday
   e) Thursday
   December

4.

Destination	Departure time
Copenhagen	11:48
Vienna	12:18
Brussels	12:58
Barcelona	13:23
Warsaw	13:53
Venice	14:28

5. Learner's own timetable.

Page 21 Polygons

1. Many possible solutions

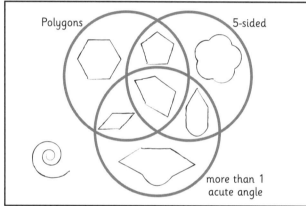

2. It is not possible to draw a kite with parallel sides, unless a rhombus is included as a special kite.
3. The angles of a parallelogram are in pairs. Opposite angles total 180°. All four angles add up to 360°.

Page 23 3D shapes and nets

1. octagonal prism
   triangular prism 4
   cuboid 3
   pentagonal prism 4
   hexagonal prism 3
   heptagonal prism 4
   If the prism has an even number of faces it needs 3 colours. If the prism has an odd number of faces it needs 4 colours.
2. heptagon-based pyramid
   tetrahedron 4
   square-based pyramid 3
   pentagon-based pyramid 4
   hexagon-based pyramid 3
   octagon-based pyramid 3
   If the base has an even number of sides then the pyramid needs 3 colours. If the base has an odd number of sides then the pyramid needs 4 colours.

3. More than one solution, e.g.:

Number of vertices	Shape
4	tetrahedron
5	square-based pyramid
6	triangular prism
7	hexagon-based pyramid
8	cube
9	octagon-based pyramid
10	pentagonal prism

4. Six possible shapes are: square, rectangle, trapezium, isosceles triangle, pentagon

Page 26 Angles in a triangle

1. All of the sides are equal. All of the angles are equal.
   No. The angles must be 60° because the total angles of a triangle are 180° and 180 ÷ 3 = 60.
2. The sum of the angles should be 180°, so the third angle should be 68°.
3. **(a)** acute **(b)** acute **(c)** acute **(d)** obtuse
   (e) acute **(f)** acute **(g)** obtuse **(h)** acute
   The angles should be calculated to be:
   (a) 33° **(b)** 48° **(c)** 33° **(d)** 114°
   (e) 66° **(f)** 66° **(g)** 114° **(h)** 33°

Page 28 Transforming shapes

1. The reflected triangle has coordinates (0, 2.5), (−1, −2.5), (1, −3.5)
2. Three of: (−4, 3), (−2, 2), (0, 1), (2, 0) (4, −1)
   The perpendicular line goes through (2, 5)
   The coordinates of the corners of the large square are (4, −1), (−2, −3), (−4, 3), (2, 5)
3. Shape D translates +2 along the *x*-axis and -4 along the *y*-axis.
   Trapezium; (−2, 2), (0, 1.5), (1, −1), (−3, 0)

Page 31 Decimals and negative numbers

1. Labels should be on the bottles in this order: 0.4 litres, 0.8 litres, 1.9 litres, 1.52 litres, 1.1 litres, 1.25 litres, 0.29 litres, 1.81 litres
2. Pairs of numbers are 0.97 and 0.03, 0.8 and 0.2, 0.7 and 0.3, 0.25 and 0.75, 0.13 and 0.87, 0.85 and 0.15, 0.1 and 0.9, 0.4 and 0.6, 0.42 and 0.58, 0.69 and 0.31.

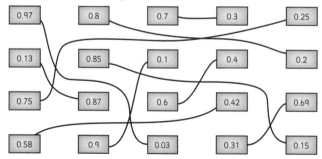

3. Aisha; Sara has earned $229.50. Aisha has earned $114.75.
4. 5 sticks measuring 0.52 m
5.

Name	Score
Natasha	−18
Safdar	−29
Isobel	−31
Ben	−33

The numbers on the ten dice should total 41.

6 Solutions depend on the outcome of the game. Compare the differences to the numbers in the learner's table.

Page 35 Mental strategies

1 Game

2 144
18 × 8 and 16 × 9
131

3 89 × 7 = 623
60 × 800 = 48 000
24 × 66 = 1584
900 × 400 = 360 000
6 × 71 = 426
17 × 7 = 119
84 × 35 = 2940
8 × 27 = 216

4 2.7 kg + 1.4 kg = 4.1 kg
0.27 kg + 0.9 2kg = 1.19 kg
0.34 kg + 0.86 kg = 1.2 kg
3.8 kg + 4.9 kg = 8.7 kg
5.5 kg + 0.49 kg = 5.99 kg
4.8 kg + 2.9 kg = 7.7 kg. The last box is labelled 7.7 kg

Page 38 Multiplication and division (2)

1

Tent A	512	460	724	106	398	714	282	538	162	804	970	598	896	732	364	192	Tent B
338	898	954	608	966	216	540	352	184	928	772	630	862	520	386	822	426	974
422	396	172	416	752	392	710	218	790	462	448	852	202	556	936	184	368	740
366	484	702	612	294	104	592	388	208	812	302	688	930	800	774	618	432	550
620	544	986	652	886	242	720	446	906	242	874	992	314	646	114	822	164	374
146	350	222	340	776	418	640	326			762	580	484	944	312	750	792	836
738	408	176	802	460	646	256	824			410	818	732	278	676	238	810	232
268	756	954	514	744	556	334	490	502	254	708	942	152	186	872	562	478	520
532	222	574	244	134	848	128	586	122	188	860	376	606	994	496	116	968	364
664	140	352	956	472	778	500	918	278	980	846	932	362	508	194	850	182	254
726	218	434	894	768	834	896	758	336	444	754	220	484	900	766	920	568	604
Tent C	628	420	292	300	266	280	908	616	998	406	362	174	780	324	884	526	Tent D

2 538 × 72 = 4304 × 9
847 × 34 = 4114 × 7

3 781 ÷ 8 = 97 remainder 5
782 ÷ 7 = 111 remainder 5
785 ÷ 6 = 130 remainder 5
788 ÷ 9 = 87 remainder 5
789 ÷ 7 = 112 remainder 5
789 ÷ 8 = 98 remainder 5

Page 41 Mass and capacity

1 All of the scales should show 465g / 0.465kg

2 All of the measuring cylinders should show 775ml / 0.775 litres

3 Three possible solutions are:
1 litre + 1 litre + 0.24 l + 0.24 l + 0.24 l + 15 ml + 5 ml = 2.74 litres
1 litre + 1 litre + 0.24 l + 0.24 l + 0.24 l + 5 ml + 5 ml + 5 ml = 2.74 litres.
1 litre + 0.24 l + 0.24 l + 0.24 l + 0.24 l + 0.24 l + 0.24 l + 15 ml + 15 ml + 15 ml + 15 ml = 2.74 litres

4 water 3.44 litres; pear 1.392 kg; blueberries 1.152 kg; yoghurt 0.608 litres

5 water 440 ml; melon 188 g; strawberries 156 g; lemon juice 36 ml

Page 44 Handling data

1

metres	yards
1	1.0912
100	109.12
200	218.24
500	545.6
1000	1091.2
2000	2182.4
5000	5456
10 000	10912

yards	metres
1	0.9091
100	90.91
200	181.82
500	454.55
1000	909.1
2000	1818.2
5000	4545.5
10 000	9091

2 275 yards ≈ 250 metres; 320 metres ≈ 350 yards

3 The bar graph should show that 25 people strongly agree, 150 people mostly agree, 50 people mostly disagree, 20 people strongly disagree and 5 people don't know.

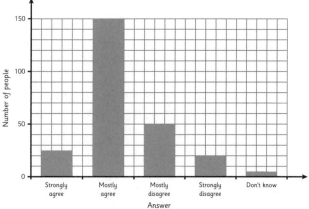

Many possible statements, for example:
Most people asked agree that the school holidays are too short.
28% of people disagree in some way that the school holidays are too short.
5 of the people asked do not know if the holidays are too short.

Page 48 Probability and averages

1 It is likely that the first person in the queue is taller than 1.3 m because 8 out of the 11 people are taller than 1.3 m.
It is impossible that the first person in the queue is shorter than 1.2 m because the shortest height is 1.25 m.
1.25 m to 1.8 m
The mode is 1.6 m
The median is 1.55 m
The mean is 1.5 m

2 F. There is an equal chance of spinning a 6 or a 1. 2 out of 4 numbers are 6.
E. It is impossible to spin a 6. 0 out of 5 numbers are 6.
F, C, D, B, A, E

3 The 20 original balls should be coloured:
4 red balls, 0 blue balls, 5 yellow balls, 1 green ball, 10 purple balls.
More than one solution to adding 4 balls, but the learner must not have added 1 yellow ball, must not have added 2 purple balls, and must have added at least 1 blue ball.

Page 51 Fractions

1

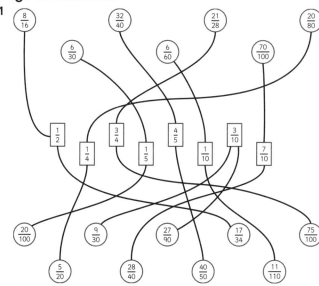

2 Player C reaches the goal.

3 Some fractions between $4\frac{1}{4}$ and $4\frac{1}{2}$ are:
$4\frac{1}{3}$, $4\frac{3}{8}$, $4\frac{3}{10}$, $4\frac{2}{5}$, $4\frac{9}{20}$, $4\frac{3}{7}$, $4\frac{49}{100}$

Page 53 Decimals and percentages

1 $50\% = \frac{1}{2}$, $25\% = \frac{1}{4}$, $10\% = \frac{1}{10}$, $100\% = 1$, $20\% = \frac{1}{5}$, $7\% = \frac{7}{100}$, $90\% = \frac{9}{10}$, $31\% = \frac{31}{100}$, $30\% = \frac{3}{10}$, $77\% = \frac{77}{100}$

2 E is the cheapest. The prices are A = $379.40, B = $379.95, C = $381, D = $380.28, E = $379.20

3 Fractions and decimals on the number line in this order:
$\frac{9}{20} = 0.45$, $\frac{24}{50} = 0.48$, $\frac{13}{25} = 0.52$, $\frac{53}{100} = 0.53$, $\frac{3}{5} = 0.6$

4 Some of the possible fractions are: $\frac{19}{25}$, $\frac{77}{100}$, $\frac{39}{50}$, $\frac{79}{100}$

5 Game

Page 55 Ratio and proportion

1 The grids with 4, 16, 36 and 64 squares can be coloured with the ratio 1:3 because the number of squares is a multiple of 4.

2 Cheng has added 10 to each ingredient. This has not kept the ratio between the ingredients the same so the recipe is different.
The quantities needed for 126 pancakes are: 1470 g (1.47 kg) flour, 21 eggs, 2520 ml (2.52 litres) milk.

3 2 in every 3, or $\frac{2}{3}$ of the fish are guppies.
1 in every 3, or $\frac{1}{3}$ of the fish are mollies.
The ratio of guppies to mollies is 2 : 1

Page 57 Metric and imperial measures

1 1 litre = approximately 1 pint(s) and 15 fl.oz
200 ml = approximately 0 pints(s) and 7 fl. oz
15 fl. oz = approximately 425 ml
2 pints and 4 fl.oz = approximately 1.25 litres

2

Name	Height	Height
Anton	1.53 m	1.53 m
Bashir	1.63 m	5 ft 4 in
Eman	167 cm	167 cm
Lily	1.50 m	4 ft 11 in
Musa	1.48 m	1.48 m
Salma	1.73 m	5 ft 8 in

3 Recipe for Onion, cheese and olive tart
Serves 20 people
140 g butter
10 large onions
10 tbsp muscovado sugar
10 tbsp balsamic vinegar
2.24 kg puff pastry
560 g feta cheese
840 g black olives
5 tbsp olive oil

Page 60 Time zones

1

Taipai							
$2\frac{1}{2}$ hours	New Delhi						
8 hours	$5\frac{1}{2}$ hours	Reykjavik					
$1\frac{1}{2}$ hours	4 hours	$9\frac{1}{2}$ hours	Adelaide				
13 hours	$10\frac{1}{2}$ hours	5 hours	$14\frac{1}{2}$ hours	Bogota			
5 hours	$2\frac{1}{2}$ hours	3 hours	$6\frac{1}{2}$ hours	8 hours	Nairobi		
$2\frac{1}{4}$ hours	15 mins	$5\frac{3}{4}$ hours	$3\frac{3}{4}$ hours	$10\frac{3}{4}$ hours	$2\frac{3}{4}$ hours	Kathmandu	
6 hours	$8\frac{1}{2}$ hours	14 hours	$4\frac{1}{2}$ hours	19 hours	11 hours	$8\frac{1}{4}$ hours	Kiribati

2 23:15 on Sunday 2nd August 2020
01:32 on Thursday 29th February 2024
22:35 on Monday 31st December 2018

3 Rosa 3 hours and 38 minutes
Mira 3 hours 51 minutes
Alma 3 hours 19 minutes
Lulu is 8 hours ahead of Rosa.

Page 62 Area and perimeter

1 The area of a rectangle is calculated by multiplying the width by the length. If the width and length measurements are in centimetres then the area is measured in square centimetres.

2 16.34 m; 41 ft; 340 mm (34 cm)

3 Approximately 65cm² is shaded.

4 Area = 384 cm²; Perimeter = 80 cm

5 A: Outer area blue, inner area red
B: Outer area red, inner area blue
C: Outer area blue, inner area red
D: Outer area red, inner area blue
E: Outer area red, inner area blue

Page 65 3D shapes

1 Missing face is the base
Number of faces: 5
Number of edges: 8
Number of vertices: 5
Name of shape: square-based pyramid

Missing face is the third side
Number of faces: 5
Number of edges: 9
Number of vertices: 6
Name of shape: triangular prism

Missing face is a triangle
Number of faces: 7
Number of edges: 12
Number of vertices: 7
Name of shape: hexagon-based pyramid

Missing face is a triangle at one end
Number of faces: 8
Number of edges: 12
Number of vertices: 6
Name of shape: octahedron

2 The learner will have made their own net of a rectangle-based pyramid.

Page 68 2D shapes and transformations

1 More than one solution. Learner should have drawn each shape on its grid and record the coordinates of the two vertices.

2 The coordinates of the vertices of the octagon are:
(0, −4), (1, −5), (3,−3), (4, −4), (7, −1), (6, 0), (4, −2), (3, −1)

Page 70 Angles

1 Learner investigation.
The learner should discover that the triangle made using the midpoints of a larger triangle has the same sized angles as the larger triangle.

2 Learner investigation.
The learner should say that the sum of the angles of a quadrilateral is 360°.

Page 73 Problems and puzzles

1 32 unshaded squares

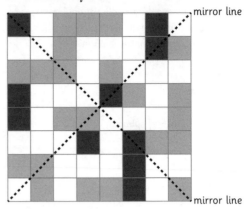

2 One plank is cut $\frac{1}{3}$ of the way along its length.
$\frac{2}{3}$ is the mean average of $\frac{1}{3}$ and 1.

3 6 pieces. More than one solution, e.g.

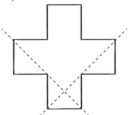

4 Some of the possible solutions are:
888 + 88 + 8 + 8 + 8 = 1000
(8888 − 888) ÷ 8 = 1000
8 × (8 + 8) + 888 − 8 − 8 = 1000

5 Solution depends on pairs of cards chosen.

6

■	▲	■	■	▲	= 42
▲	▲	●	●	●	= 36
●	▲	□	■	●	= 37
■	●	●	●	▲	= 35
●	●	▲	■	■	= 37
= 37	= 39	= 37	= 36	= 38	

7 (a) 25
   (b) The number of fruits is always three times the year number, then subtract two.
   (c)

Year	8	10	20	50	100
Number of fruits	22	28	58	148	298

   (d) 134th year.

8 1st place Jasem, Numberfuns, 2
2nd place Maria, Geometers, 3
3rd place Eman, Dataists, 1
4th place Tomas, Calculots, 4